# Living with a Diabetic Partner

## A Saga of Overcoming the Odds

# *Living with a Diabetic Partner*

## *A Saga of Overcoming the Odds*

**Nalini Tandon**

Published in 2024 by Notionpress, India

E-mail: nmtandon@gmail.com

Living With a Diabetic Partner



Cover designed by Pratibha Pandey, Artists/Designer

ISBN : 9798896321057

This book is lovingly dedicated to my husband Prabhat Narain Tandon, who despite his problems, sustains my morale, and is my champion and tower of strength in this journey of life.

# Table of Contents

Troubles in life come in all
Shapes and Sizes

# Author's Note

Life is a tapestry woven with unexpected experiences, some of which alter its entire course in unimaginable ways.

The inspiration for writing this book sprang from one such transformative event that unfolded in my life.

In moments of adversity, we often find ourselves overwhelmed with fear, confusion, anger, and despair. We question the heavens, wondering, "Why me?" Little do we realize that life is a meandering caravan of events—some leave indelible marks, while others merely pass by like fleeting memories. When a profound event struck our lives, we too were deeply disheartened. My husband could not fathom the full extent of how this event would impact him, and I, despite my medical background and daily interactions with patients and their struggles, found myself unprepared to face the practical challenges that ensued. Looking back now, we can chuckle at the irony and tragedy of it all, but in those days and months, detachment was far from our minds.

This book aims to recount our journey through the highs and lows of living with the uninvited "third partner" in our lives. It is a story of resilience, growth, and the remarkable ability of the human spirit to adapt to the unexpected. While navigating the complexities of life, both personally and professionally, we discovered invaluable lessons that transformed us in ways we never thought possible.

As you delve into these pages, I hope our experiences resonate with you and provide solace, guidance, or simply a reminder that even in the face of uncertainty, there is strength to be found in embracing life's unforeseen twists.

May this memoir be a beacon of hope for those facing their own trials, reminding them that within the tapestry of life, every thread, no matter how unexpected, adds to the beauty of the overall masterpiece. This book is an attempt to describe some aspects of our life and how we coped with events that were often dispiriting, and occasionally, even life-threatening. Life has endowed us with a multitude of blessings, as you will find out, though this book is dedicated to a narration of some of the problems we faced in our journey.

Every human being has a tale to tell because our stories are unique. This is our story! I hope you will like going through it and may perhaps learn from it while enjoying the trials and triumphs of this journey.

**Dr. Nalini Tandon**

# Prologue

When God created human beings, He also planted tests (roadblocks) in their life's journey to keep them on their toes, searching, learning, and discovering ways to pass (overcome) these tests. The afflictions that human beings acquire on the path traversed on this earth are part of God's tests. One of these afflictions is diabetes mellitus.

Diabetes mellitus is a disease in which people suffer because of the inappropriately increased levels of blood sugar in their body. More than 530 million adults, between the ages of 20 and 80 years, currently live with this disease. It is one of the fastest growing afflictions in the world, and each year, about 7 million people are added to the list of diabetics. Rapid and major lifestyle changes are said to be an important cause of this epidemic.

The countries of South Asia together account for 60% of the population of the world afflicted with diabetes. Out of this population, Indians comprise approximately 88% of diabetics. Statistics collected and shared by the International Diabetes Federation in 2020 indicate that there are 77 million persons diagnosed with diabetes in India, up from 22 million in 2016. The prevalence rate increased by approximately 9% during this four-year period. At this rate, it is expected that the number of diabetes patients in India will rise to more than 134 million by 2034. However, it is also envisaged that more than half this number is undiagnosed. About 25 million people in India have prediabetes, and without adequate dietary control, exercise, and other precautions, this number is liable to convert into those with diabetes. The number of diabetes patients in India is higher in the southern states as compared to central Indian and north Indian states.

Indians tend to develop diabetes at a lower Basal Metabolic Index (BMI), which means that they are liable to develop diabetes even if they are not overweight or obese. Studies also indicate that they are liable to develop this affliction at a younger age than their Western counterparts, for they have a higher genetic propensity for diabetes and increased insulin resistance. The number of Type 1 diabetes patients are comparatively fewer in India, and the majority have Type 2 diabetes.

The Government of India has launched an Indian Diabetes Prevention Program and a National Diabetes Control Program. Both these programs employ the techniques of lifestyle modification, treatment with the drug metformin, and health education. Despite this, about 5% of the surveyed population was unaware of their diabetic status, as per surveys conducted by the National Institute of Health and National Family Health Survey. In addition, there is also the propensity among

Indians to believe that their diabetes is under control without undergoing regular checkups. Another important factor is that the use of traditional and herbal medicines, besides modern drugs, is very prevalent in India for the treatment or control of diabetes.

The reasons for the unprecedented increase of this debilitating disease in India can be attributed to rapid urbanization, which has led to a more sedentary lifestyle, the rising trend of eating out and consuming readymade and fast food, long working hours and reduced physical activity, all of which result in weight gain. The three culprits for the increasing incidence of diabetes can be summarized as obesity, weight gain, and an unhealthy lifestyle. Indian diets are high in carbohydrates and low in proteins. Moreover, many Indians are vegetarians, which makes adequate protein intake challenging. Add to this the upsurge in alcohol consumption, and you have a formula for substantially escalating the chances of developing lifestyle diseases like diabetes.

There is an urgent necessity to bring about a change, and the first step in this direction is the consumption of a balanced diet. From my experience of over 40 years, I can safely relate to the advice given by expert dieticians and would counsel people to follow a diet rich in proteins and greens and low in carbohydrates.

People who have diabetes should also take their medicines at regular intervals and follow a fixed, age-appropriate exercise routine. They should consult a dietician and follow their advice.

Those caring for diabetics and staying with them must be vigilant and conscious of their special needs, guiding and encouraging them to follow the right lifestyle. By adopting these simple changes, one can lead a comfortable and fruitful life.

We must realize that once it arrives, this unwanted visitor stays for life, and we must learn to live with it, bending to its requirements, intimidating, cajoling, and coping with its tantrums.

# The Stomach Affair

*"If life were predictable it would cease to be life and be without flavor."*

—Eleanor Roosevelt

"I have a request," he said to me quietly.

"What is it?" I asked, expecting him to ask me out.

It was February of 1972. My future husband had come to meet me. We had met for the first time in January that year, although we had been watching each other from afar for quite some time at his aunt's house—his aunt's daughter was married to my cousin, and I often went to meet my cousin's family.

To my utter surprise, he said, "I have constant stomach problems. I often suffer from diarrhea or constipation. Can you please get my stool tested?" To say that I was taken aback is an understatement.

I was a final-year medical student at the time, and collecting samples to get them tested at pathology, microbiology, or biochemistry laboratories was part of my training. It was not a problem for me, but the request from my future fiancé was a shock. The romance had not yet begun, and it was getting mired in earthly routine. Anyway, I conceded, and the next day Mr. Prabhat Tandon, my would-be fiancé, handed a sample of his stool to me. I accepted it with a wry smile; not flowers, but a stool sample for me!

The results revealed that he had giardiasis and amoebiasis. It turned out that those creatures loved his gut and liked to play hide-and-seek there. This was a common complaint amongst my patients. The diagnosis soon flitted away from my mind, replaced by the rainbow colors of the courtship days of my life. We roamed the streets of Connaught Place, hand in hand, surviving on never-ending chit chat and stories of our lives until then. Occasionally, cold coffee at Volga's or hot coffee at Coffee House helped to dissipate the rumblings of our poor alimentary canals.

Soon, it was time to celebrate. We got engaged on July 5, 1972, and tied the knot on January 22, 1973, settling down to enjoy the variegated hues of matrimony.

Before I proceed with this tale, let me tell you a secret. I love food, especially good food, which during those days meant junk food and not its distant cousin, healthy food. I did not know, however, that my husband was just the opposite. I could eat at any time, and midnight snacks were more the norm than freak accidents, while he was a fastidious eater, surviving on a strict schedule and specific healthy foods because of his delicate stomach and gastric constitution. We do not talk about these practical differences during the rosy days of courtship, but the colors dissolved into black and white soon enough.

During our honeymoon, we traveled by road from Udaipur to Mount Abu. I was hungry when the bus stopped near a *dhaba* (a roadside tea-stall). The aroma of hot *pakoras* and *samosas* teased my nostrils, and anticipation sharpened my rumbling appetite. My husband went to the street stall and returned with six bananas. I looked at him questioningly, "Where are the *samosas*?"

He calmly explained, "This is the only safe and healthy food item. They have so much fried stuff!"

Can you imagine the depth of my disappointment? That was the first inkling I had of the stomach affair, and a tiny bit of the rainbow flitted away from my heart.

As we settled down to our domestic life, I learned a little more. From childhood, a daily breakfast of bread, butter, milk, tea, and occasionally, eggs, *parathas*, and *jalebis* were my staple food, so I was unfamiliar with the concept of fresh breakfast prepared daily. Despite having spent a large chunk of his teenage years, almost the entire 1960s, in hostels, my husband wanted a freshly cooked breakfast from a menu of *poha*, black gram, moong dal, and other healthy food. I was a novice but eager to develop my culinary skills. Thus, I obliged him by learning to cook his preferred meals, gradually mastering the art enough to prepare them tolerably well.

Of course, there were disasters. Once, I put potatoes to boil in a pressure cooker and forgot to add water. The angry cooker revolted by melting down the valve and becoming black and blue inside. Another time, I laboriously cut okra and placed it in a cooking vessel. I put the vessel on high heat and forgot about it while I enjoyed the evening breeze on the terrace. The poor okra was charred beyond recognition, and I was in tears. I knew that water should not be added while cooking okra, but I did not know that it had to be cooked on low heat. But the bane of my life was milk. It loved boiling over and creating a mess in the kitchen just when I had turned my back. Perhaps it enjoyed the spectacle of my horrified and bewildered face.

Slowly and steadily, however, I acquired the requisite expertise, and such accidents became fewer.

One day, my husband returned from the office, looking troubled. I too had just returned after my internship duties and was tired. As we settled down, each of us holding a cup of warm tea, I asked him what was troubling him. He hesitantly whispered, "I have noticed a swelling in my groin. Can you examine it?"

"Of course," I answered.

It turned out that he was fearful of consulting his office physician and had very reluctantly discussed this problem even with me, after debating about it for two days. I examined him and concluded that he had a right-sided inguinal hernia. My diagnosis, I was amazed to find, made him extremely morose, and he did not talk to me about it for the next four or five days. He was depressed. As a doctor, I did not find his diagnosis earth-shattering, so I failed to understand his behavior. He was the patient, fearful of the unknown and scared to undergo an operative procedure. I had to employ all my persuasive powers to take him to a specialist, who explained further and gradually allayed his fears.

Things settled down eventually, but this was my first encounter with the various medical problems I would be facing in future with the person I loved — the person who was my life partner. How was I to envisage any of it? It took me almost a year to convince my darling to agree to a corrective surgery.

Owing to his delicate stomach and gastric constitution, my husband always wanted fresh and simple food, served at fixed times. I thus developed the habit of cooking everything fresh, trying to provide tempting variations in food. I have become so accustomed to it that even today, the first thing I do is to plan and cook a fresh dish for breakfast. My daughters often make fun of me, watching me near the stove each morning, but now, this deep-rooted habit is difficult to change.

Perhaps my husband's stomach issues arose because he was an extremely fast eater. If we did not sit down to eat together, he was apt to finish eating even before I had begun. During the early days of our marriage, I used to prepare food lovingly and serve him hot chapatis, hoping that he would wait for me to join him. But no! By the time I arrived at the table with my chapati, he would have finished his food and would be calmly walking toward the wash basin to wash his hands. Ultimately, this exasperated me so much that I stopped serving him food till everything was ready, including chapatis for both of us. Only then would I lay the table so that we could eat together. Despite this, he would often get up before I had finished eating. He would stay back when I complained, but he was so uncomfortable that I invariably ended up asking him to go and wash his hands. Life mellows you, and over the years, he too has slowed down. He eats quite slowly now, chewing, relishing, and enjoying his food.

My darling husband, Prabhat, has another habit. He does not like very hot food. Food must be fresh and warm; piping hot food irritates him. When my elder daughter was about four months old, Prabhat's sister-in-law, his brother's wife, had come to help us out because I was doing my housejob (equivalent to first-year residency), and an infant requires constant care. We had not managed to hire reliable full-time help, and there was no creche or day-care center at my hospital. When I was at home, I took care of my daughter and Bhabhi (sister-in-law) cooked the evening meal. She insisted on serving my husband first and eating with me later, which was the custom at my in-laws' place in Bareilly. One day, she served him hot dal, a piping hot vegetable, and then a hot chapati right off the griddle. Bhabhi did not know it, but this was a recipe for disaster. My dear husband was so angry that he left the table and walked out. Bhabhi was at a loss and could not comprehend what had gone wrong.

He later slinked sheepishly, his anger abated. Bhabhi then inquired about the reason for his tantrum. He sat down to eat and then calmly stated, "The meal was too hot. Please do not serve me piping hot food; it burns my tongue." He then firmly announced to my flabbergasted sister-in-law that hereafter she should prepare the entire meal and the three of us would eat together as he did not like eating alone. Although I was a little annoyed with him for walking out in a huff, I almost hugged him in delight when he announced that we must eat together. I too dislike eating without him, and till today, enjoy having meals with family.

Thus, our life progressed. Over time, he became extremely busy with his job and I with my patients. Our family increased from two to three and then from three to four. We booked our own DDA apartment and eventually moved there in February 1981. We also employed a reliable and efficient full-time maid. We were happy and satisfied so far, unaware of the clouds on the horizon.

<u>Diabetes: an overview</u>

Human beings eat carbohydrates, fats, and proteins in the form of food ingested in the body throughout the day. In normal circumstances, we can utilize all the food that enters our body by converting it to energy, which is used instantly or stored in the body for future use. The chief source of energy is glucose, and the chief supplier of glucose is carbohydrates, supplemented by proteins and fats.

A person with diabetes is not able to carry out this function efficiently. So, what is this diabetes which disrupts our crucial body functions?

The scientific name of this disease is diabetes mellitus. "Diabetes" is a Greek word meaning "to siphon off," while "mellitus" is a Latin word meaning "sweet." To understand this disease, one needs to comprehend the production of energy in the body.

The energy is provided by carbohydrates or glucose ingested as food or drink, but this process requires the help of insulin. Insulin is a hormone produced by the Islets of Langerhans, (named after the scientist who discovered them), which are a part of the pancreas, an organ in the abdomen that undertakes many crucial functions. The islets of Langerhans are just one part of the pancreas. Beta cells in these islets produce insulin, which helps the cells of the body to use the glucose circulating in the blood and convert it into energy to maintain various bodily functions. Moreover, excess glucose is also stored in the cells. It is thus removed from blood circulation, and blood sugar levels remain normal.

A person has diabetes mellitus, or diabetes in short, when there is lack of adequate insulin in the body. This can be due to two reasons:

1. The beta cells produce inadequate or no insulin.
2. The insulin produced is ineffective, that is, the body cannot use it properly.

If the function or production of insulin is disrupted, blood sugar builds up in our body, raising our blood sugar level. Over time, if it remains untreated, the high blood sugar level can damage our nerves, eyes, kidneys, heart, and other organs and systems.

# The Precursors

*"It does not matter how slowly you go as long as you do not stop."*

—Confucius

We received the gift of our second daughter in November 1977. She was a sickly child, suffering from a series of ailments, chiefly of the upper respiratory tract. My attention was therefore on her and her welfare. By this time, I was also quite acclimatized to my husband's gastric problems. However, the devil still prevailed and could not be ignored.

Soon after shifting to Saket in February 1981, where we had purchased a DDA apartment under the Self-Financing Scheme of the Delhi

Government, we consulted a medical practitioner, a specialist in general medicine, who was a friend's husband. He prescribed a new medicine to Prabhat for his constipation for six months, and my husband started taking it. Noticing that he was not benefiting much from it and his problems in fact increased a little, I requested him to stop the medicine after three months. I was afraid of its adverse side effects, and I could not lay my hands on the scientific details about this drug. Those were not the days of computers and Google, at least not in India.

Seeking to overcome the never-ending gastric issues that pervaded my husband's life, we also tried various natural remedies for them. His chief problem was frequent constipation;

—the day he was not able to empty his bowels properly, he suffered from bloating, loss of appetite, and other ill effects of constipation. This resulted in irritability and loss of sleep. Among the natural remedies that helped my husband was eating *bel* or *bael* fruit (stone apple or Bengal quince in English). The ripe pulp of this fruit or a cold drink made from the ripe pulp benefited my husband to a great extent and allowed him to have a satisfactory bowel movement every morning.

*Bel* is available in Delhi during summer, from March to July. This barely covered half the year, and for the rest of the year, his suffering returned with a vengeance, making him uncomfortable and sometimes irritable. We consulted several physicians and gastroenterologists, but nothing seemed to help him.

The problem was ultimately resolved by my cousin Puneet, the son of my father's younger brother. Puneet is at present a renowned gastroenterologist in Lucknow. While he was doing his fellowship in the early 1990s, we met him at a family wedding in Lucknow. Marriages in India are occasions for meeting all of your relatives, socializing actively, and exchanging notes as well as gossip. We thus met several cousins with whom we had not been in touch. Among them were Puneet and his wife, Dr. Sangeeta.

As is common in India, while conversing with Puneet, my husband casually asked, "What should I take for my constipation? It is a constant problem for me."

"Start taking Naturolax with water, once or twice a day," was his reply. He went on to explain that Naturolax is a type of natural fiber, like Isabgol.

I was listening and interjected, "He has been taking Isabgol quite often, but it has no effect. What you are suggesting is the same thing."

Puneet explained, "Naturolax is the powder form of Isabgol, and it has been proven to be more effective in cases of chronic constipation."

Though not fully convinced, my husband agreed to try it. The results were very effective, very similar to the satisfaction felt after consuming *bel*. This remedy has continued to this day. My husband consumes it once or twice daily, one teaspoon with two glasses of water, and finally, this simple but effective treatment managed to assuage the stomach affair substantially.

Life is never without challenges, however. After we moved into our new apartment in Saket, we found that the house was infested with cockroaches and crickets. This set of apartments was built on land acquired from farmers, and pests infesting the farmland still lingered. The crickets were so destructive that we soon had holes in our new curtains. The cockroaches were all over the kitchen, in the storage cupboards, in the sink, on the kitchen platform, and in the corners of the floor. If I happened to wake up at night to get something from the kitchen, the moment I switched the light on, I would find the slinky creatures having a gala time, prancing around, feasting on the crumbs on the floor and leftovers in the dirty utensils in the sink. They crawled and scurried all over the place, in all colors and sizes, leaving me disgusted and nauseated.

Unable to control these unwanted guests, we contacted a pest control agency after due research and gave them the contract to de-bug our house. The agency personnel would come once a month and spray the entire house with pest control reagents. Prior to their arrival, we had to empty the kitchen and cover everything well. We were out of the house for almost six hours, and when we returned, all utensils had to be washed and every surface cleaned, not only in the kitchen but also throughout the house. The treatment continued for more than a year. The crickets disappeared, though we had to replace the curtains. The cockroaches were hardier, but their presence was minimal.

During this period, we tried to visit our parents at least once a year, albeit at different times. With young children, we constantly needed to take time off from work, so we barely managed about a week's leave to visit our parents. In October 1983, we went to Bareilly, his hometown, to meet his parents, siblings, and their families. Apart from us, all his brothers lived together in the ancestral home in Bareilly. We combined our visit with the Dussehra festival, thus trying to save some paid time off.

Alas, that was not to be! The day after we arrived, my husband was down with a fever. Thinking it was just the seasonal viral attack, I was a little nonchalant. However, the fever became a serious affair. It came with its own agenda and went on a rising spree, deciding to settle at levels of 103–104 degrees Fahrenheit. No medicine seemed to work, and the fever continued its dance within his body, unabated. Laboratory tests did not indicate any positive specificity. Local doctors were consulted in vain. Finally, the fever came down on the tenth day, leaving my husband and the entire family exhausted, physically, and mentally. We returned home thereafter and resumed our respective jobs.

A few weeks after our return, on November 11, 1983, my husband's elder brother, Ganesh Bhai, passed away after a very brief illness of just two days. This was a big shock to the entire family. He was seven years older than my husband and closest to him in age. He had two young sons, one of whom was just three years old.

These family issues and the major and minor blips in life perhaps prepared me for what was still beyond the horizon. Such incidents, which are interwoven in our lives and our stories, grant us the strength to face bigger hurdles. I was to recall each of these events later, as I tried to untangle the threads of the webs enmeshing our lives. Were they the precursors to what was yet to come?

## History of Diabetes:

Available records suggest that humans have known about diabetes mellitus probably since 250 BC. However, an ancient Egyptian papyrus of 1550 BC mentions a disease where the patients were passing urine very frequently.

The sweet taste of urine or presence of sugar in urine has been mentioned in the texts of several ancient civilizations, such as the Indians, Greeks, Egyptians, Chinese, and Persians. However, Ayurvedic physicians are credited with noticing and mentioning it first in the 5th–6th century BC.

Ancient Indian literature refers to this disease as *madhumeha*. *"Madhu"* means *"honey,"* while *"meha"* in Sanskrit means "passing urine or making water." Although in Hindi the word *"meha"* has come to mean rain, the term *madhumeha,* given by the great Indian healer and scholar Sushruta, literally meant "sweet urine." Mention of this disease is found in *Sushruta Samhita Volume* 2. Patients in India were initially diagnosed by noticing that ants collected around their urine. However, no special treatment has been mentioned in the available ancient Indian literature.

Besides India, the medical literature of other great civilizations also mentions this disease. The Chinese called it "Xiaoke" meaning "wasting thirst." The term "diabetes" was given to this disease by the great physician Aretaeus. He was born in Cappadocia, which is presently part of Turkey, but was then a constituent of the Greek empire. Aretaeus, in 2 AD, described this disease in detail and coined the word "diabetes." The word "mellitus" was added much later, in 1675, by Thomas Willis. Though "diabetes mellitus" literally means "passing sweet urine," in this disease, excess sugar is found in both the urine and the blood of patients.

In the 10th century AD, a Persian physician, Avicenna, provided a detailed description of both diabetes mellitus and diabetes insipidus. The two conditions are very different, and this differentiation was discovered and enumerated in the 18th century AD by the German physician, Johann Peter Frank. Diabetes insipidus occurs because of hormonal imbalance. It is a rare disorder where the body makes and passes too much urine.

A patient with this disease feels intensely thirsty and urinates very frequently, but the blood sugar is normal, and the patient does not pass sugar in urine. It is unrelated to diabetes mellitus.

# The Bombshell

*"Life is made of ever so many partings
welded together."*

– Charles Dickens

By the end of 1983, all my brothers and sisters were married, except my sister Pankaj. The entire clan was desperately trying to find a suitable match for her, but she had already rejected several proposals. She turned 30 in April 1984, and we had almost given up the idea of her marriage. However, providence had other plans, and in May 1984, she accepted a proposal from Jagdeep. My parents and the rest of the family sighed with relief.

Pankaj's engagement took place at Allahabad in July, and the wedding was fixed for October 3, 1984. The dance of the holocaust in our lives commenced thereafter.

My uncle (my father's youngest brother and Puneet's father), who had no health-related issues until then, was diagnosed with a cancerous brain tumor in September 1984. The entire family was in shock, especially my father, who was extremely distressed even though he maintained a stoic silence. The marriage had been scheduled, and my uncle, who was very enthusiastic about this marriage, also insisted that it must be performed as planned. We decided to host the marriage in Delhi, from our place, as the boy's family lived close to our residence and it would be convenient for my parents.

Gradually, the guests started arriving. Indian marriages are a conglomeration of customs spread over several days in which all relatives participate. In fact, the more, the merrier!

A day before the wedding, my husband said to me, "Please get me a glass of water." I obliged.

Fifteen minutes later, he called me again. "Get me a glass of water, please".

I was busy and did not pay much heed to his demand, simply giving him another glass of water.

A little while later, I saw him going to the toilet, after which he asked me for another glass of water.

A miniscule thought began nagging me.

"You've been asking for water very frequently and using the toilet quite often. We need to get your blood sugar checked," I told him.

The house was full of guests, and I was running hither and thither to organize everything. My husband was also similarly busy, and both of us forgot this conversation. The next day, October 3, dawned bright, and the marriage ceremony and events went off smoothly as per schedule, much to our relief and happiness.

Meanwhile, my uncle's condition was deteriorating rapidly. He was being treated at Lucknow and my parents were anxious to visit him. My brother made their travel arrangements, and they departed for Lucknow on the morning of October 4.

Both my husband and I had taken time off from work for the wedding. We spent the day of October 4 wrapping up things and saying goodbye to departing relatives. After dinner that evening, everyone was in a buoyant mood but extremely tired, and we went to bed to enjoy a well-earned rest.

The vibrant tintinnabulations were reverberating in the room. The persistently annoying sound kept troubling me. I thought I must be dreaming, but someone shook me. I opened my eyes reluctantly.

"What?" I inquired, annoyed at being woken up so rudely.

"The telephone is ringing," someone whispered in my ear. Very reluctantly, I got up and headed towards the phone. We had recently installed a landline phone. The era of mobile phones had not arrived in India.

"Hello," I said softly to not disturb others.

The voice at the other end was unfamiliar, but what I heard shook me to the core, driving away any remnants of sleep.

"Jagdeep has met with an accident," the voice informed me.

"Who are you?" I asked, trying to prevent my head from spinning.

"I am his friend, and we work together at Maruti," the voice confirmed.

"Where is he?" I further probed.

He went on to explain that he was speaking from the emergency center of Wellington Hospital (now known as Ram Manohar Lohia Hospital).

"Is my sister there?" I asked to confirm the genuineness of the call and he handed the phone to Pankaj, who was crying.

Any thought of sleep had flown away by now, even though I had barely rested for 15 minutes. The news felt like a bad dream, and my mind was refusing to register the reality. I woke my husband and brother and apprised them of this latest development. By this time, several other family members were also awake. Giving them the facts in brief, the three of us left for the hospital, where we learned that Jagdeep had been taken for an X-ray. My sister clung to me, sobbing inconsolably. Somehow, we managed to calm her down.

This was their first night together, and they were supposed to spend it in the honeymoon suite of Akbar Hotel. It transpired that Jagdeep and Pankaj had decided to attend the marriage reception of a friend and were planning to retire to Akbar Hotel from there. While at the reception, Jagdeep, desiring to present my sister with a *gajra* (flower decoration for the hair), had gone to Connaught Place (now

Rajeev Chowk) with a friend on his two-wheeler. While returning, a car had hit them from behind. Jagdeep, who was the pillion rider, fell on the road and fractured his leg.

Life's ways are perverse, and situations change in the blink of an eye. Just last night, at the posh Akbar Hotel, we had all celebrated the sacred marriage vows taken by Pankaj and Jagdeep. Within 24 hours, we were at a hospital casualty, worried about the future. We did not know that there was more on the horizon, lurking behind the clouds.

Jagdeep's elder brother had reached the hospital, so we returned home with Pankaj, consoling and reassuring her that it was only a fracture and would heal soon. Little did we know that fate had other plans. Our parents had reached Lucknow, and the next morning, we gently broke the news to them.

Despite two nights of almost no rest, my husband had to go to work that morning. He was due to leave for a work trip to Belgium, and it was imperative that he complete the essential paperwork. While preparing his lunchbox, I requested him to consult his doctor at the office clinic and get a slip for the requisite tests. He followed my advice, and his doctor ordered that his blood sugar levels be tested. Owing to shortage of time, as he was to leave within 3–4 days, we went to a nearby laboratory at Panchsheel Park the next morning, where he gave his blood sample. We went to collect the report together on the evening of October 6, and the bomb exploded.

The doctor met us in his office. He was well known to me and was the husband of one of my teachers. Handing the report to us, he admonished my husband, "You are not taking care of your blood sugar."

My face went pale when I saw the readings: 300 fasting and 450 post meals. I felt nauseous; this was a Macbethian moment for me.

Dr. Sachdeva inquired gently, "Is this the first report?"

I barely nodded my head in the affirmative. He then kindly explained to my husband, "There is nothing to worry about. The sugar levels will come down with treatment."

I was numb with anxiety, but my husband was blissfully unaware of the implications of this diagnosis. He was under the delusion that the problem would be solved with medication. He did not know that diabetes is a life sentence.

One of the doctors from his office lived close to our residence. From the laboratory, we went straight to his place to show him the report and tell him that my husband had to leave for Belgium on the morning of October 9. The poor man was in a dilemma. His advice was that Prabhat should not go and must start his treatment, but my husband did not want to miss the trip. Finally, the doctor compromised, "I can allow you to go if your wife goes with you. She is a doctor and will have the responsibility of monitoring your diet and medicines." I was taken aback, but both of us agreed to this proposal.

I had just two days to complete all the formalities and get permission from my office. Luckily, my office personnel were extremely cooperative, and expediting official procedures, granted me the letter of approval. We had to arrange for someone to be with our daughters while both of us were out of the country. Fortunately, we had a reliable full-time maid, and one of our relatives agreed to be with the girls.

Our trip to Belgium passed without incident, and we have pleasant memories of it tucked away in photo albums and in our hearts. However, that month was like the waves of an ocean passing through our lives, some bringing droplets of happiness and others wreaking extreme havoc.

By the time we returned from Belgium, Jagdeep was back home from the hospital and he, along with Pankaj, was living with his elder brother. Their house was in the block next to ours.

A couple of days after returning from Belgium, we met the doctor friend who had been treating my husband for his gastric ailments. This person examined his eyes and declared, "You have Grade 3 diabetic changes in your eyes. Start the necessary treatment immediately, or you will lose your eyesight." To say that we were shocked is an understatement. I am a constant worrier, and this declaration sent my imagination into a downward spiral of complex worries, imagining my husband to be going blind very soon. My saner mind and medical knowledge kept admonishing me to think logically, but I was beside myself with anxiety.

A day later, we received excruciating news from Allahabad. My youngest sister, Neerja, had met with an accident and had a serious head injury. She was in a coma and was being shifted to Lucknow for further treatment. Was there no end to tragedies? My mind was in a whirl: Should I rush to Lucknow or wait to get my husband's eyes checked by a specialist, which was due in two days? The dilemma was mind-numbing. I wonder even today if it was the right decision, but I stayed back with my husband.

The ophthalmologist examined my husband's eyes and the retina and declared, "Your eyes are perfectly normal. Diabetic changes begin only 10–15 years after developing diabetes. They can be controlled and delayed with good control of blood sugar." We heaved a sigh of relief. Fortunately, the same evening, we received the news that my sister had regained consciousness and was on a slow but steady path to recovery, without needing an operation.

Sometimes in life, it does not rain, but it pours! My poor parents were besides themselves with worry. My uncle was serious, and all their three daughters were facing serious problems. The month of October 1984 was teetering on the edge of disaster, but fortunately changed its mind at the last moment. However, I cannot end this piece of adventure without mentioning the postscript.

On October 31, Indira Gandhi, the then Prime Minister of India, was assassinated at her residence. There was mayhem and utter chaos in Delhi for three days. Several noble, gentle, and innocent Sikh lives were lost in the citywide riots. The excellent orthopedic surgeon who was treating my brother-in-law, Jagdeep, also fled from the city. Jagdeep's family consulted another doctor at Kapoor Memorial Hospital in Delhi, who operated on Jagdeep's leg as the bones were not healing. I humbly advised against the operation—the previous orthopedic surgeon had also given the same opinion. The bones tibia and fibula were fractured at the lower end, where the blood supply is low and healing takes longer than normal. However, the bones do heal, and any lingering defect can be corrected through proper footwear.

Who can fight destiny? Jagdeep's foot was operated upon at the end of December. The surgery went well, but everyone overlooked one crucial point. It is these minor mistakes that often cause the loss of lives in the medical field. Apparently, Jagdeep had not been vaccinated in his childhood and had never received an anti-tetanus vaccine. At the Ram Manohar Lohia Hospital, he was given one dose of the vaccine, probably as a precautionary booster since it was a roadside injury. No history was taken regarding his vaccination status either at the first hospital or at the second one, nor was he advised to take a repeat injection after six weeks. The doctors who attended to him at Kapoor Hospital completely neglected or forgot about this crucial point.

The third day after his operation, I received a phone call. A hesitant but ominous voice at the other end introduced itself as the doctor who had operated on Jagdeep. Fumbling over his words, he informed me, "Mr. Jagdeep has neck pain and is finding it difficult to speak."

"What do you think is the problem? Is there an infection?" I inquired, baffled by this phone call.

He again stated quietly, "He is complaining of a stiff back."

Suspicion dawned on me, and my body prickled with fear. Inhaling sharply, I asked pointedly, "Do you suspect tetanus?"

"Yes," came his reply, confirming my worst fears.

This was really a bolt from the blue. He informed me that the patient was being shifted to the tetanus ward of LNJP Hospital, as no facilities were available at the current hospital. It fell on me to inform my sister and all the relatives. Once again, within three months of marriage, Pankaj was facing a calamity in her life.

Jagdeep's condition teetered from bad to worse for a fortnight. Meanwhile, my uncle passed away on January 14, 1985. Slowly but steadily, Jagdeep fought back the demon called tetanus, his body clawing its path to recovery. He was discharged after a month, but he took years to recover and regain his health, the fractured leg continuing to trouble him frequently. We thank the Lord to this day for bestowing his life back to him.

## Diagnosis of Diabetes

**Diabetes is diagnosed based on the patient's symptoms and a series of urine and blood tests. A patient is declared as suffering from**

diabetes when the level of blood sugar remains persistently high above the prescribed normal range.

## Symptoms:

Patients may complain of weight loss, excessive thirst, increased appetite, and increased frequency of urination. They may also complain of sores that don't heal or take too long to heal, occasional blurry vision, dryness of skin, tingling in the extremities, and more fatigue than normal.

They may have all or some of these symptoms.

Occasionally, patients may have no symptoms but may be gaining weight, though usually this is not considered a symptom. All of this indicates that diabetes is a complex disease.

<u>Tests done to confirm a diagnosis of diabetes mellitus:</u>

1.  A simple urine test called Routine urine test will indicate the presence of glucose in urine.

2.  Blood tests for testing the level of glucose in the blood will indicate the presence of levels higher than normal:

    a.  Tests done after a fast of 8 hours or more will show a blood sugar level of more than 110 mg/DL.

b. Testing of blood sugar randomly at any given time may indicate a level of more than 200 mg/DL.

c. Testing of blood sugar after two hours of consuming a meal (known as postprandial or PP testing) will indicate a blood sugar level of more than 140 mg /DL.

A person is labeled a diabetic based on the complaints, symptoms, and blood sugar levels.

# The First Aftershock

*"All the world's a stage, and all the men and women are merely players."*

—William Shakespeare

The darkest clouds tend to disperse after a while. There seems to be no light while they are there and despair fills the heart, but then, slowly, the dawn breaks, dispersing the despair, bringing forth a flickering smile to the lips. Human beings have the immense capacity to adapt to every situation life throws at them. We too learned to adjust to diabetes, cope with life, and live with it. Gradually, my husband also realized that he must live with this ailment, and it is a lifelong affair. The doctors had tried various drug treatments for him, but he did not respond well to those drugs. They had then started him on insulin. We learned to test, inject, and continue with life.

In India, the moment you talk of an ailment troubling you, everyone tends to become an expert doctor, spouting forth a cocktail of advice. Everywhere we went, my husband was also admonished to try another set of medicines or a different diet.

"You must eat bitter foods like *karela* and *neem*. The bitterness will dissipate the sugar, and you will be well," someone declared.

"You must eat drumsticks and dishes made from its flowers," another well-wisher surmised. As an aside, drumstick flowers are very bitter, and although people do eat them as a cooked vegetable, I had never seen them in our households, neither at my mother's nor at my in-laws' place.

There were others who advised him to eat guava, guava leaves, *jamun, jamun* seed powder, fenugreek seed powder, and other such food. My husband was fed up with all the well-meant counsel. He has always believed firmly in science and scientific evidence–based advice, so he refused to follow any of these recipes. At one point, exasperated by all the different foods being suggested to him, he laughingly stated, "I should become a monkey, jumping from tree to tree, consuming leaves, flowers, and fruits."

One day, we received an invitation to attend the *mundan* (hair-shaving) ceremony of his cousin's son, followed by lunch. It was a working day, so neither I nor the children could go. My husband had managed to get leave, so he decided to go along with another cousin.

They returned from the ceremony at around 5 P.M. We were all back home by then, and the maid was cooking dinner. His cousin stayed back to chat, and they were laughing and talking in the drawing room.

Suddenly, I heard my husband call me, "Neeloo, please come here."

Expecting to learn some juicy titbits from the day's events, I entered the drawing room. He appeared to be serious and confused and told me, "I am seeing everything double." I was surprised but not alarmed at first.

I am ashamed to admit that I had forgotten that diplopia was a sign of low blood sugar. My husband had just experienced his first attack of hypoglycemia. It appeared that the food he ate at the party was the rich fare usually served on such occasions. To keep his blood sugar under control, he had not eaten much, and he still wasn't eating much with the drinks he and his cousin were enjoying.

This was a mild attack and soon dissipated after he ate properly. However, it was the first aftershock for us, mandating us to pay attention to all the aspects of this third life partner we were being forced to live with. How unaware we were of the tantrums to be thrown by this compulsory guest!

## History of Treatment of Diabetes

**Although the condition of a diabetic patient has been described as early as 1500 BC by the Egyptians, and later by the Indians, Chinese, Middle Eastern Islamic world and Europeans, proper treatment eluded humankind until the early 20th century.**

**The early Egyptians prescribed herbal treatments directed more toward the kidneys, because it was considered a disease of the kidneys.**

In the 5th and 6th century BC, Sushruta and Charka, two ancient Indian physicians, prescribed dietary remedies for diabetes. They were also the first to describe two different types of diabetes.

The Chinese described the disease as the "three increase and one loss": increase in urination, thirst, and hunger, along with loss of weight. However, no specific remedy was prescribed other than herbs for the treatment of urinary troubles.

Mayan literature indicates the use of the leaves of a plant called *Bauhinia divaricata* to treat such patients.

Thus, before the mid-1800s, herbs, bloodletting, and sometimes, opium was the treatment for diabetes mellitus. In fact, some physicians prescribed extra nourishment as patients lost weight, and excessive consumption of sweets often led to the death of patients. Later, John Rollo, a Scottish military surgeon, recommended fasting and a diet of meats and fewer carbohydrates, and the results were better.

By 1797, scientists had conducted tests with pancreatic extracts, which raised hopes of finding a treatment for this elusive disease. Toward the end of the 19th century, two German scientists further confirmed that the pancreas was the site producing a substance that controlled the management of sugar in the body. Throughout the 18th and 19th centuries, scientists in the western world persisted in their efforts to solve this mystery. Ultimately, in 1922, Banting and Best were able to extract insulin from the pancreas of a dog. It was then that the modern treatment of diabetes mellitus really made progress.

The tablet metformin, still successfully used in the treatment of diabetes, was also developed in 1922–23. Since then, many new drugs have been introduced by pharma companies and scientists for the successful management of this disease.

# The Diet Challenge

*Jaisee pare so sahi rahe, kahi Raheem yeh deh,*

*Dharti hi par parat hai, seet ghaam aur meh !!*

*(Live with this body of yours, says Raheem, no matter what befalls it, just like the earth lives and thrives in cold, heat, and rain.)*

– Raheem

I have always been a disinterested cook. My cooking was just sufficient to feed the household, interspersed with fits of enthusiasm for some recipes that occasionally turned out well. Diabetes, however, forced me to pay more attention to the kitchen. I was lucky to have an excellent full-time maid during the early years of this period, so I could focus on preparing food that suited my husband's palate as well as his diabetes. I started with gathering the tools.

The doctors insisted that his meals should be based on a fixed calorie intake. However, measuring the various ingredients was a problem. I had managed so far with rough measures of a fist, bowls, or ladles, but now, buying a measuring scale for the ingredients had become a necessity. Next, I added measuring cups and measuring spoons. The scientist residing in my husband insisted that I measure and weigh the exact amount of flour required for each chapati, so that I did not overfeed him. Similar accuracy was followed for lentils, rice, and vegetables. This system had one major drawback, however: My husband was not the only member of the family. I had two lively, young daughters who needed variety as well as nourishment in their meals, and revolted against eating the same drab fare every day, both at lunch and dinner.

Necessity is the mother of invention. I had no choice but to get different types of meals prepared for them, but this did not last long.

After a few months of this culinary evolution, my husband was admitted to the All India Institute of Medical Sciences (AIIMS), a premier medical institute of Delhi. AIIMS was established under a Special Act of the Parliament of India, known as the AIIMS Act of 1956. At present, it has around 2,500 beds and provides services in nearly all the major and minor medical specialties and super-specialties, catering to patients from all over the world. It is well known in India and abroad for its excellent facilities. My husband was under the treatment of the endocrinologist, Dr. Kochupillai, who wanted to try some different medicines on him. But more on this AIIMS adventure later.

One good outcome of this episode was that the dietician at AIIMS presented me with a book of recipes and recommended diets for diabetics. She had written the book in collaboration with Dr. MMS Ahuja, head of the Endocrinology Department at AIIMS.

The book was a boon. It had multiple exchange measurements and exchange recipes for vegetarian and non-vegetarian dishes, mainly Indian fare. Over the next few years, it became my bible for cooking different types of meals for my family. The drabness and tastelessness of my cooking was a thing of the past as these recipes added some spice to life, literally! I could provide North Indian and South Indian meals without disturbing the delicate balance of the diabetic menace.

Another requirement to manage diabetes that all doctors insisted upon was increasing the amount of protein in my husband's diet. Regular Indian cuisine, especially if it is vegetarian, lacks protein. Although both of us ate non-vegetarian food, we were products of strict vegetarian households and had grown up on the usual North Indian *dal-roti-sabzi*. We loved it and thrived on it. Non-vegetarian dishes provided occasional variety, but only if none of our parents or in-laws were staying with us, when even garlic and onion were taboo.

We were now forced to think of our meals from the protein perspective. Our family friend, Mr. Seth, suggested fish, which he declared to be the best source of protein. He was a Bengali and ate fish daily. He very generously offered to buy fish for us and did so religiously once a week for almost two years. I had no idea what to do with fish. Although his wife and daughter gave me lessons, I ended up making only pan-fried fish. My daughters hated the bones in the fish (it turned out that Bengalis love their fish with bones), but something was better than nothing.

I gradually learned to make some chicken and mutton dishes and even tried my hand at making mutton kebabs, though, regrettably, I have never excelled in it.

Next came a time when someone at my husband's office enlightened him about the devastating effects of dairy products, especially milk, advising him to drink soy milk instead, which is a richer source of better-quality protein. My dear husband, who usually ignored well-meant dietary tips from all and sundry, somehow believed this one.

The catch was the procurement of soy milk, for it was not as commonly available back then as it is today. Coincidentally, one of our neighbors was a couple whose son was allergic to lactose.

A van came every week to deliver soy milk for their child, and they gave us one carton to try out the taste. Unlike me, my husband is not a fussy eater when it relates to health, and is ever willing to follow dietary restrictions if they have health benefits. I am sure he did not like the taste of soy milk, but he agreed to switch to it. Unfortunately, the product outsourcing division of the firm informed us that the van could only supply us with soy milk if we bought at least two cartons of ten boxes each weekly. It was impossible to consume so much milk, so the plan fizzled out. However, the decision to give up dairy milk remained instilled in my husband's brain.

My experiments with soybeans thus commenced. With great enthusiasm, we bought a kilogram of dried soybeans. I soaked a cup of these beans. The next morning, the outer transparent covering of the beans had to be removed. Little did I know what I was in for! The more I rubbed, the more stubborn the covering became, fluffing up with water but refusing to part ways. I must have rubbed and washed for more than an hour, wasting several liters of water, to fully remove all the covers. But victory was mine at last, for all the covers were finally removed.

The next step was to grind the beans in a mixer-grinder. Luckily, this process was easy. Finally, I had to extract milk from this paste by squeezing it through a thin/cheese cloth. My husband and my children helped to extract the milk. Voila, the milk was finally ready! It was boiled and tasted, and the unanimous verdict was that it had come out to perfection. I was happy that love's labor had not been lost. I continued to repeat this laborious process for the next four months or so. I tried to make tofu from this milk. It turned out to be perfect, though the yogurt prepared with it was a disaster.

When my husband visited his doctor after four months, he narrated the soybean saga to him. The doctor laughed and told him, "Please go back to dairy milk. There is no harm in it." Thankfully, that was the last of our adventures with soybeans.

However, our adventures with his meals and calorie intake continue to this day, though he is the expert now and manages his intake himself. He, and thus I, lead a life of fixed meals at stipulated times. It is often an irritant to others, despite everyone's best efforts to be accommodative.

## Insulin

**Insulin is a natural hormone produced in our bodies inside the large gland called pancreas. The pancreas is an important organ, and one of its crucial functions is to produce insulin. The hormone is secreted by the islets of Langerhans in the pancreas. In some people, various medical factors cause the body to**

develop resistance to insulin, making it ineffective or less effective.

The islets of Langerhans were first described by Dr. Paul Langerhans, a German physician, in 1869 and are named after him.

Insulin is produced by the beta cells in the islets of Langerhans, a part of the structure of this complex gland called pancreas. The islets also have alpha cells and delta cells, but insulin is produced by the beta cells.

These cells release insulin in two ways. A small amount is continuously produced, like water dripping from a leaking tap. A greater volume of insulin is released when there is an increase in the glucose level in the body, for example, immediately after a meal. The function of insulin is to facilitate the uptake of glucose by the cells of the body and thus provide energy.

Think of a trapdoor. Each cell of the body has a trapdoor through which the glucose, present and circulating in the blood, can enter. Glucose is the energy required by the body to function. The body receives its supply of glucose through meals and through production in the liver.

The trapdoor of the cells will open when insulin is present. Thus, insulin becomes the magical "open sesame," which opens the door and provides the requisite energy for the body to function. This is true for all parts of the body except the brain, where the uptake of glucose can occur directly.

Insulin is also the key to differentiate between Type 1 and Type 2 diabetes.

In Type 1 diabetes, the patient's body is unable to produce insulin. The beta cells of the islets of Langerhans in the patient's pancreas shut down and stop producing insulin. This could be due to an autoimmune reaction in the body, the body's own immune system attacking and destroying the beta cells. The cause for this immune reaction could either be genetic factors or environmental factors, such as a viral attack. The end result is that insulin is not available to meet the demands of the body.

Consequently, the food the patient ingests cannot be processed and converted into energy. The blood sugar levels rise, and the patient is said to be diabetic.

In Type 2 diabetes, on the other hand, the beta cells produce insulin, but for some reason, this insulin is ineffective, and the person is said to have developed insulin resistance. Due to this insulin resistance, in these patients too, the body is not able to process glucose and supply it to the cells as energy to ensure proper functioning of the body. The exact reason for developing insulin resistance is not known, but it could be due to environmental, genetic, or lifestyle factors.

# Testing and Coping

*I slept and dreamt that life was joy. I awoke and saw that life was service. I acted, and behold, service was joy!*

– Rabindranath Tagore

"Mummy, the color is yellow again!"

This virtuous declaration emanated from the bathroom, where my younger daughter was huddled with her father.

She was referring to the color of urine. Since my husband had been diagnosed with diabetes and prescribed insulin, our life featured urine testing at least twice a day, along with all its heartaches and tensions. Diabetic patients have to compulsorily keep testing and checking their blood sugar to maintain the delicate balance between food intake and medication. This is imperative for patients who are on insulin, as there is a high chance of their blood sugar plummeting to dangerous lows. In accordance with these rules, soon after his diagnosis, my husband started testing his urine to monitor his blood sugar. We were all learning.

As a medical student and resident doctor, I had collected innumerable samples of urine. I had also tested many samples that required instant results and could not await the final diagnoses from the pathological lab. However, I was now realizing the difference between diagnosing a patient and conducting the same test, day in and day out, on my husband's urine.

Our home had become a mini laboratory. Being a meticulous worker with implicit faith in science and its magical potency, my husband collected all the paraphernalia as soon as the doctor announced regular testing. Test tubes, test tube stands, test tube holders, spirit lamp, spirit, cotton swabs, Benedict's solution—everything was lined up in our mini laboratory. Our house was small, so my medical books gave room to all this equipment. Our little flat often presented the weird appearance of an ill-managed laboratory. Accidents were bound to happen—glass tubes broke, spirit bottles spilled, or worse, were empty, matchboxes would be found swimming in buckets, hands got burned, and the urine spilled. It was an exasperating, messy affair because we did not have proper counters or adequate space.

Testing was done with punctilious exactitude, however, every morning and evening, with another test or two thrown in when required. My young daughters watched over my husband like hawks, and the results were conveyed to me with delighted or awestruck announcements, like the one I had just heard.

This was India in the early 1980s, and we had no access to devices like a glucometer. Packaged alcohol swabs were also unheard of, and everyone used cotton and liquid medical alcohol or spirit to wipe and clean the skin.

Even the insulin prescribed to my husband was not human insulin; it was a porcine or bovine variety.

In the beginning, my husband fervently believed that with regular and careful treatment, he would be completely cured of diabetes. As time progressed and he learned more through reading and discussion with his doctors, he realized that it was a lifelong malaise, and he was stuck with it. Well, his indomitable spirit came to his assistance, and he decided to live with it with grace and honor. Thus, our house had evolved into a laboratory for constant testing, evaluating, and coping. Highs and lows, both of our moods and his blood sugar readings, were the norm.

Good days brought forth sighs of pleasure, and bad days came with bouts of depression.

Gradually, with India opening its doors to the world in the 1990s, many scientific assets entered our mini laboratory. The first of these were Uri sticks, small packets of paper sticks that liberated us from several tools, such as spirit lamps and test tube holders. The freedom from the need to heat the urine with Benedict's solution was most welcome. The color reflected in a Uri stick dipped in the urine held in a test tube served the same purpose. The various colors seen in test tubes were now available for reading and understanding on the thin, linear paper strips.

Our overcrowded bathrooms must have heaved a sigh of relief.

The next step was the availability of glucosticks, followed very shortly by the glucometer. The first glucometer we managed to get hold of was very different from its sophisticated cousins now available so readily. It was bulkier and heavier, but it was a heaven-sent (not science-sent) blessing for us, and we were elated. We no longer needed to mess with urine in the house!

Although the glucometer was available, we could not get hold of pricking pens. So, the finger prick was done by using a sterilized needle each time blood sugar had to be tested. Sometimes, when a sterile needle pack was not readily available, we sterilized the needle in the primitive way, by heating it to a glowing red color on the gas stove. Alcohol swabs too were an unknown commodity back then, and we stacked bottles of methylated spirit and bundles of cotton. The only treatment for my husband's diabetes was insulin and constant testing, balanced with the management of calories and food. Believe me, it was a delicate dance that the entire household had to practice, perfect, and endure.

With liberalization, major foreign drug and medical equipment companies entered the Indian market. More sophisticated glucometers of different varieties became available and commenced their entry into our household. Diverse pricking equipment was also available, and as we moved into the next century, insulin pens became the norm. All of these developments made our lives, especially my husband's life, easier. Being an enthusiastic scientist, he missed no opportunity to acquire any new item available in the market, understand its use, and utilize it fully.

When alcohol swabs appeared on the horizon of the Indian medical market, we acquired them without delay. They have become a necessary fixture in our household since then, and the insulin pens have slowly morphed into their present extremely convenient versions that my husband uses. Like the bathrooms, our medicine cabinet also danced with pleasure, as we got rid of the bales of cotton, bottles of blue spirit, and dozens of insulin syringes. It was now lined with boxes of alcohol swabs and a couple of insulin pens and their cohorts.

My life with a diabetic partner thus evolved from urine test tubes to glucometers, glass insulin syringes to insulin pens, and cotton bundles to alcohol swabs.

We continued regular monitoring, but his blood sugar readings were not satisfactory. The diabetes was labile, wavering from high to low. We consulted different doctors, ultimately reaching the prestigious AIIMS. It was a bit difficult to penetrate the corridors of power, but we persisted and achieved success. We started consulting Dr. Kochupillai, a very senior doctor in the Endocrinology

Department. He was a knowledgeable and well-informed doctor.

In September 1985, he advised my husband to get admitted so that he could try different oral medications on him and closely monitor their impact. We acquiesced, and my husband was admitted to the endocrinology ward. A private room was not available, so he was given the side room of a general ward. He was not happy, but he coped. I took leave for a week and careened between home and hospital.

My husband's diet was strictly monitored, and he would eat only the hospital-cooked food prescribed by the dieticians. Dr. Kochupillai put him on a variety of oral medications, trying out each of the drugs in use. However, my husband's body failed to respond, and the high levels of blood sugar persisted. On the fifth day, when the readings reached as high as 400, the good doctor gave up. He discharged my husband with the impressive diagnosis of non-insulin dependent diabetes mellitus (NIDDM). To this was added the postscript of "not responding to drugs." We thus returned home, back to the routine of injections and testing. My husband had been very hopeful of getting rid of the daily injections and monitoring of blood sugar two to three times a day, but that was not to be. We braced ourselves for a lifetime of injecting, testing, and coping.

Meticulous delving into the medical history of the family and extended family failed to elicit any diabetic relatives. Yet, my husband had the most brittle type of this common chronic ailment. There was nothing to do but bow to the will of God or to chance, according to my nonbeliever husband. Dr. Kochupillai advised him, and emphasized every time we met him, that no matter what the world did, my husband must exercise and eat his meals at regular times, carefully monitoring the content and quantity. My meticulous husband made this his mantra and follows it to this day.

## Types of Diabetes

Diabetes is diagnosed when the level of blood sugar remains persistently high above the prescribed normal range. Diabetes results when there is a lack of insulin in the body, or the insulin that is present in the body is unable to act properly because of the presence or lack of certain factors.

There are two main classifications of diabetes :

1. Insulin-Dependent Diabetes Mellitus (IDDM): In this case, the body is unable to produce insulin because of genetic or non-genetic factors.

2. Non-Insulin Dependent Diabetes Mellitus (NIDDM): Although the body produces insulin in this case, the hormone is not able to act properly and perform its function owing to several factors.

As the research and study of this disease progressed, scientists have identified several other categories of diabetes:

a) Prediabetes: This is the stage before diabetes. In prediabetes, the patient's blood sugar level is on the higher side, but it is not high enough to be labeled as diabetes.

b) Gestational Diabetes: Some women develop high blood sugar during pregnancy, which generally recedes to normal levels after delivery. Some women, however, continue to suffer from diabetes.

c) Type 3C: A person is said to have this type of diabetes if there is damage to the pancreas due to disease or the person has undergone pancreatectomy for some reason.

d) Latent Autoimmune Diabetes in Adults (LADA): It occurs usually in people after the age of 30 years, and is caused by an autoimmune reaction. It is a type of Type 1 diabetes.

e) Maturity Onset Diabetes of the Young (MODY): This tends to run in families and is said to be due to the mutation of an inherited gene.

f) Neonatal Diabetes: It is found in infants within the first six months of life. It may be transient and recede, or it may persist throughout life.

g) Brittle Diabetes: It is a kind of Type 1 diabetes in which the patient suffers from very frequent episodes of high and low blood sugar levels.

Diabetes can also develop if the body has become resistant to insulin. The exact cause of someone developing resistance to insulin is not known, but when that happens, the body cells fail to respond and are unable to create energy from glucose despite the availability of insulin.

However, in any kind of diabetes, the chief cause is either the lack of insulin or its inability to effectively perform its function.

# I Shall Join the Ganga and the Brahmaputra

*If you are going through hell, keep going!*

— Winston Churchill

Diabetes may be a friend or foe, but it is with you for life, filling the days with a variety of experiences, especially if you or a loved one has been endowed with diabetes that has to be controlled with insulin, irrespective of its original cause and diagnosis. It has its pros and cons, but the cons disrupt life as soon as one becomes complacent. It was no different for us.

It was a lazy summer evening in May 1986, and the family had just finished dinner. We always dined early, a habit that was strengthened when diabetes entered our household. My husband wanted to rest after dinner, so he went to bed. After about 10 minutes, I went to say something to him, and he stared blankly at me. I asked him to get up, but he curled up his legs and said he was unable to move them. I suspected that his blood sugar had plummeted below normal. However, he had just had a full meal, so this situation indicating signs of low blood sugar was very puzzling. What I did not recall then was that this situation could occur if the pre-meal blood sugar had been very low, and the meal did not include any food (sweets or fruit juice, for instance) that would raise blood sugar instantly.

Unfortunately, I did not have my stock of glucose injectables on hand. Thus, instead of wasting time on testing his blood sugar level and procuring glucose injections, we decided to take him to hospital. His body was stiff and he was unable to straighten his legs, so my daughters and I could not lift him. Fortunately, my brother was at home. He carried my husband to the car, and we drove to AIIMS, 7 km from our house.

Midway to the hospital, my husband sat up and began to talk normally. Relieved, we turned around to return home. I discussed this puzzling episode with my friends and his doctor later, and the conclusion was that his blood sugar must have been very low before the evening meal. He had been able to eat normally, but since there was no sweet food in the dinner to raise the sugar level more rapidly, the meal took longer to digest and raise his blood sugar back to normal. It was a scary lesson for me and made me overcautious about his health.

I am a constant worrier and have bouts of acute anxiety. You can surmise my apprehension after this episode. I immediately replenished my stock of glucagon injections, syringes, and needles, and arranged for an intravenous drip that I could administer at home if required. These precautions were often a boon during the early years of living with my diabetic husband.

Between 1985 and 1990, my husband had several episodes of hypoglycemia, many of which occurred at night. As glucose tablets were not available at that time, I would stock plenty of glucose biscuits or sweets at home. I am a very light sleeper. The low sugar warning generally woke me up when his tossing and turning in bed increased. When it was a milder attack, I fed him glucose biscuits, and waited for 15–20 minutes for them to take effect. You must recall that we did not possess a glucometer then. Sometimes, by the time I was awake, his sugar would be very low. He would thrash all over the bed, his eyes wild and his lips pursed tight, stubbornly refusing to take any food orally. I had no recourse but to inject glucose at these times. I generally woke up my daughters to help me steady him and hold his hand so that I could find a vein and inject the lifesaving fluid.

During such episodes, my husband would talk wildly. My daughters were very young at that time; the younger one had not entered her teens yet. Though they must have been scared, they bravely faced the situation and became adept at helping me. Necessity is the mother of invention.

On one such occasion, my husband was uncontrollable. He kept thrashing around the bed, declaring that he was working on the Ganga project and would join the Ganga and Brahmaputra rivers. When my younger daughter, Geetanjali, tried to help, he shouted and kicked at her, asking her to get out, although miraculously he allowed the elder daughter to help. Geetanjali was in tears and very scared. My daughters and I were not able to hold him still or feed him, and injecting glucose became an impossible task.

Time was running out, and fear clutched my heart. It was 3 A.M. I knew I needed help. Braving the night and keeping my fears to myself, I asked my daughters to keep an eye on their father and went out to ask my neighbors for help. One doctor couple, the Mahajans, live behind our house. I walked to their flat and rang the bell. I was very apprehensive about disturbing them in the middle of the night. However, they were very courteous and helpful. After two rings of the bell, Dr. Mahajan woke up, and on hearing my tale, he got dressed immediately and accompanied me. We were able to start the glucose drip with his help, and within a few minutes, my husband calmed down. I thanked Dr. Mahajan profusely. He was a godsend that day. I fail to comprehend how we would have managed otherwise.

Such episodes were part of our daily life during this period. Once, my husband and I were returning from a relative's house, and my daughters were at home. My husband was driving, and he started speeding suddenly. I kept requesting him to slow down, but he was in the throes of another attack of low blood sugar even though he had partaken tea and snacks 15 minutes ago. I had thought that all would be well, but I was wrong. His blood sugar must have been very low, and the amount of food he had eaten could not prevent the attack.

To continue the tale, my husband kept speeding, and instead of turning toward the house, he drove straight ahead. I had a hand on the steering wheel to steady him, but he kept brushing me off, and I was afraid we would meet with a major mishap soon. I kept beseeching him to stop and prayed with all my heart. Ultimately, the inevitable happened, but God had heard my prayer. He crashed into the midline divider and instinctively applied the brakes. The car stopped and the jolt somehow helped, for in a small lucid interval, he realized that his blood sugar was low.

By this time, as happens in India, a crowd had gathered around us. I took out the sweets that I always carried, and thankfully, my husband ate them, simultaneously moving over from the driver's seat to the passenger side. The crowd, unknown to us, had assessed the damage to the car. They declared that it was drivable as only the side bumper had been damaged. I took the key, sat in the driver's seat, and drove home, sending innumerable thankful prayers to the Almighty.

Our entire household had now come to terms with diabetes, insulin, and hypoglycemia. Each of us had become adept at recognizing the first signs of low blood sugar in my husband and immediately warning the others to take preventative steps. Such episodes still occur because with insulin treatment, maintaining equilibrium between food, exercise, and medication is like a delicate dance. If the patient tries to cut a fine edge, they are apt to succumb to attacks of low blood sugar. If they are not so careful, the readings may go haywire, and they could suffer from the aftereffects of persistent high blood glucose levels.

## Complications of Diabetes

**Diabetes affects the entire body, literally from head to toe. Patients most commonly suffer from the following complications:**

1. <u>Diabetic Nephropathy</u>: Diabetes affects the kidneys, and if uncontrolled, causes a change and depletion in their function. Statistics indicate a slight fall in the incidence of this complication, but it is still a major threat, especially in patients with poor control of blood sugar levels. Patients may develop oedema in the feet and other signs of fluid retention. Changes in kidney function can be detected early through testing for albuminuria.

2. <u>Diabetic Retinopathy</u>- Changes in the retina are seen in long-term diabetics. These changes develop insidiously over a long time. Regular eye

checkups of diabetic patients are therefore extremely important so that any changes can be detected at the earliest. Poor glycemic control will lead to early development of these devastating changes as patients can go blind.

3. <u>Diabetic Neuropathy-</u> Neuropathy means damage to the nerves due to the persistent high levels of glucose circulating in the blood. Neuropathy occurs because of diminished blood flow to the peripheries. Diabetic patients, especially those who have had the disease for a long time, with poor control of blood sugar levels, develop this complication. It can be

peripheral neuropathy that affects the limbs, most commonly the lower limbs, causing tingling, numbness, pain, loss of sensation, and occasionally, in severe cases, skin ulcers. It can also be autonomic neuropathy affecting the internal organs, such as the digestive system, kidneys, and sex organs. Patients must be examined for any signs of neuropathy, and they must be educated about self-examination for any suspected signs.

4. Diabetics, especially long-term diabetics, are prone to developing heart problems. These occur due to atherosclerosis, that is, the hardening

of arteries. People who are overweight, smoke, or have poor control of blood sugar, high blood pressure, and high cholesterol levels are more prone to developing heart complications.

5. The other complications that can occur with long-term diabetes are stroke, liver damage, fungal infections, problems of the oral cavity, and hearing loss.

# Coming Back to Life

*Maati kahe kumhaar se tu kya raunde mohe,*
*Ek din aisa ayega, main raundoongi tohe!*
*("Who are you to trample upon me?" says*
*the mud to the potter.*
*"There will come a day when I will be the one*
*trampling you.")*

—Kabir Das

Life has astounding ways of testing you by throwing unimaginable unforeseen circumstances at you. One such incident in our life was again related to my husband's diabetes.

In February 1987, my husband's senior colleague, Mr. Srivastava, who was retired and working then at Sana, Yemen, visited us. He was also my brother's father-in-law, and we had immense respect for him, both as a person and as a senior colleague. He asked my husband for an imprint of both of his palms since he wanted to consult someone—an expert in palmistry—about my husband's illness. He loved my husband as his eldest son and was proud of his achievements. My husband does not believe in such predictions, but he could not say no to Mr. Srivastava. So, he gave the impressions of his palms on paper.

When Mr. Srivastava returned to Sana, he sent us an urgent message to consult a doctor immediately—the prediction was that my husband might suffer from an acute, life-threatening heart attack soon. I am a superstitious person and was quite perturbed. However, as a doctor, I could not find anything disturbing in all the investigations that were conducted. His blood pressure (BP), ECG, and blood reports were all within normal limits. We were thus lulled into complacency, dismissing the urgent bulletin from Sana.

Disaster struck 15–20 days later, around March 10. My husband is a person of habit and rarely deviates from his routine. On that day, however, he did not return from the office at his usual time. He used to travel to his office by a chartered bus, and the bus always returned at the appointed hour. My husband walked from the drop-off point and would be home by 5:30 P.M. Several other colleagues also traveled with him. I telephoned one of his colleagues to check whether the bus had been delayed. As soon as I learned that the person I had phoned was at home and the bus had come and gone, I got worried. I telephoned other colleagues, and all of them verified that my husband had been on the bus and should have reached home.

I was panicking, and in desperation, I dialed the police. They scoffed at me, saying it was just 15 minutes past the regular time and he could have gone to the market. Luckily, I had help at home that day. Leaving the girls with her, I grabbed the stethoscope, BP apparatus, and glucose injections and drove to the local market. There was no sign of my husband there. I then telephoned a few of his colleagues, nearly in tears, and asked for their advice on what I should do next. All of them confirmed that they had seen my husband on the bus when it started, and since they did not see him after his scheduled stop, they were sure he had alighted. They were all aware of his health problems and hypoglycemia attacks. It was decided that we would drive to the place where the bus was parked for the night and make further inquiries with the driver. I drove my car and Mr. Sinha, Mr. Seth, and Mr. Bala, my husband's colleagues who lived in the neighborhood, accompanied me.

We drove to Green Park. The Indian Oil building of today was not in existence then. The empty lot was used to park buses, and the chartered bus was parked there. While I waited in the car, the three gentlemen went in search of the driver. I was alone in the car, praying fervently. I remember thinking, "Has

God granted me just 14 years of life with my husband?"

Luckily, the three gentlemen found the driver. He told us that when he had parked the bus, there was a gentleman lying on a seat. "I asked him to get up as the bus was to be locked. He got off the bus with his bag and went toward the bus stop. He must have been a little drunk as he was walking in a wayward manner."

My heart fluttered with fear when I heard this. This was a sure sign that my husband was in the throes of hypoglycemia and was not aware of his actions. If he had taken a bus, we would never be able to find him. The three gentlemen, though worried, were saner in their reasoning. They decided that we should check the Emergency wards of AIIMS and Safdarjung Hospital, both of which are very close to Green Park. They reasoned that someone might have taken him there as he was unable to walk properly.

I drove to AIIMS. We parked and went to the Emergency. I personally went around, gazing at every patient. Ultimately, a young doctor, noticing my tear-stained face, asked how she could help. On becoming aware of the details, she scanned the list of patients admitted in ER in the past two hours and informed us that no such patient had arrived. She assured us that if my husband were brought in later, she would take care of him. She also telephoned the Emergency ward of Safdarjung Hospital and learned that no such patient had been brought there either.

We were now at a loss about what to do next, and I was openly crying. Mr. Bala then suggested that we drive again toward Green Park, very slowly, so that all three of them could scan the pavements and the roads. Unable to use my own mental faculties, I complied, and we started driving to Green Park from AIIMS, at a very slow speed, keeping as close to the pavement as possible. And then, the gods had pity on me.

As we neared the crossing just opposite the Uphaar cinema entrance, my co-passengers asked me to stop. They had noticed someone lying under the *neem* tree on the pavement. I stopped and looked, and there he was, lying under the tree, his briefcase under his head. He was lying very still, but his eyes were open. Fear clutched my heart. All three gentlemen scrambled out of the car and picked him up, gently stretching him out on the back seat. The two gentlemen who had to travel on the backseat adjusted themselves in the space available, one with my husband's head on his lap and the other managing my husband's legs.

I made a U-turn and sped to AIIMS again, this time stopping at the ER doors. My husband was wheeled inside, and luckily, we met the same doctor who had helped us earlier. I filled her in about his medical details while she started an intravenous glucose drip. Within 15 minutes, my husband opened his eyes and surveyed us, though he took some time to comprehend the situation and his surroundings. The only good thing about a hypoglycemic attack is the magical speed with which it responds to glucose.

My husband was discharged within 30 minutes, and we returned home with him. All the way home, I silently kept thanking the Almighty for His benevolence. On reaching home, my husband was helped inside, and only then did the three angels (I call them angels, because they were that to me on this fateful day) depart. I thanked them profusely for all their help, and I am grateful to them till this day. Without their assistance, I would never have been able to locate my husband on that fateful day.

I was extremely puzzled about the reason for this acute episode of hypoglycemia. I had provided my husband with sufficient food for his office hours. Besides the breakfast at home, he had a couple of fruits to eat after two hours. His lunchbox contained dal, chapati, rice, curd, and vegetables, along with salad. Lastly, I had made him sandwiches, which he was supposed to eat just before leaving the office so that the kind of mishap he had suffered could be avoided.

When I discussed the episode with him later, he vehemently asserted that he had eaten all the meals. The cause of this episode remained a mystery, and after discussion with his doctor, the only conclusion drawn was that perhaps his body did produce some insulin that day.

The prediction made by that palm reader in Sana came true. We did face a critical emergency, almost a death-like situation, within the time he stated, though not in the form he envisaged.

## Methods of Treating Diabetes

1. <u>Dietary control</u>: **This is the most important aspect of controlling or treating diabetes. An intricate balance must be maintained between intake and output. Diabetes is a disease in which the pancreatic cells have become**

ineffective in producing insulin, or they produce insufficient or impotent insulin. Bringing them back to their normal state has not been found possible. Thus, curing this disease is not the aim, and controlling it is the direction of treatment. Careful monitoring of the ingestion of food is thus the mainstay of diabetic management.

2. <u>Measurement of blood glucose levels:</u> This should be regularly done at home and at the laboratory when advised by the treating doctors. The level of glucose in the blood indicates the well-being of the patient and is

therefore extremely important. As far as possible, patients should themselves check their blood sugar at home regularly. Sophisticated instruments, equipment, and devices are now available for home testing. The blood sugar levels should be maintained within the prescribed limits.

3. <u>Maintenance of body weight</u>: Unusual weight gain or loss is not desirable, and patients must consult their doctors if this is noticed.

4. <u>Control of blood pressure</u>: Diabetes affects all the systems of the body. To prevent unwanted side effects on the heart as well

as other systems, it is important to regularly check the blood pressure and ensure that it is under control.

5. <u>Regular and proper intake of medications:</u> The patient may be prescribed insulin or drugs or both. It is important to follow the doctor's instructions and regularly take the medication.

6. Checking of glycated hemoglobin (HbA1c) at prescribed intervals

7. <u>Yearly eye checkups:</u> This is important because long-term diabetes can cause changes in the retina and patients may lose their vision.

8. <u>Exercise:</u> Regular exercise, yoga, or walking for at least 30–40 minutes daily or a minimum of 30 minutes every alternate day is effective in controlling diabetes.

9. <u>Treatment of any underlying pathology</u>: If a patient has an infection or other comorbidity, it is important to treat it simultaneously and effectively. This is mandatory to ensure proper control of blood sugar.

Treatment of diabetes is a holistic maintenance of all the bodily functions rather than just popping pills or taking injections.

# Break the Door

*The real test is not whether you avoid this
failure, because you won't. It's whether you
let it harden or shame you into inaction, or
whether you learn from it; whether you
choose to persevere."*

—Barack Obama

"Bua, Phoophaji is not opening the door."

I heard these words as soon as I stepped out of my car with all my office paraphernalia. Amit, my cousin's son, staying with us temporarily because of his new job, stood near the door, bewildered. He had returned from work about five minutes ago and could not get in because the door was locked from inside.

A familiar ominous fear enveloped my heart as I rushed to him. The outer mesh door was closed, but the inner wooden door was open. Through the open bedroom door inside, we could see my husband sitting on the bed. He was alone at home. Both my daughters were studying in the US at this time, one after marriage, and the other still single.

"Phoophaji is sitting there, but he is not coming to open the door!" Amit could not understand the problem, but I did. My husband was in the throes of a hypoglycemic attack.

Despite the strict instruction to not latch the door from the inside but only lock it with the key, my dear husband had forgotten and had latched the door from the inside. Now, he was unable to get up and open it, being helpless when the menace of low blood sugar shrouded his mind and body.

I rushed to the nearby market to summon help. We are lucky to have a market in our block, and help is readily available in the form of various types of mechanics. A mechanic came with me and helped to get the latch opened from the outside without needing to break the door down.

I was getting increasingly desperate with each minute of this task. I explained the situation to a baffled Amit, who then pitched in and ensured that the door was opened as quickly as possible. No sooner were we inside than I grabbed the glucose injections and injected my husband with the lifesaving liquid. I did not wait to try oral sweeteners because I was not sure how much time had elapsed.

The year was 1999, and a similar episode had occurred a few months earlier. I was working as the Deputy Medical Commissioner at the Employees State Insurance Corporation (ESIC) headquarters. I invariably left work a little late and was rarely home before 6.30 P.M. One day, my husband returned early from work. After reaching home and partaking in some snacks, he went off to rest. Unlike these days, he was not in the habit of checking his blood sugar frequently then. So, he ate and went to sleep.

By the time I returned from the office, he was deep in the clutches of an attack of low blood sugar and could not answer the doorbell. The wooden front door was latched from the inside. I knew he was back from the office because we had talked on the phone. Mobile phones were a novelty then, and our conversations were generally on landline phones.

I became very agitated when he failed to open the door despite my repeated loud requests and telephone calls. I knew he was suffering from an attack of low blood sugar and required immediate assistance, but I was unable to reach him. By this time, several of my immediate neighbors and some shopkeepers from the nearby market were aware of my husband's problems. Hearing me call my husband's name repeatedly, the neighbors came to my aid. One of them brought a couple of mechanics from the market, and I asked them to break open the door. However, they asked me to be patient and assessed the situation. I was getting desperate by the minute. Each second was crucial for my husband's survival. Ultimately, the mechanics decided to try and pry open the screws attaching the door to the door frame. This would remove the two adjacent portions together, and we would be able to get in. We did not have a steel door at that time, so this method appealed. The doors would not be broken and could be screwed back again.

The tools were collected, and the doors were unscrewed, removing the hinges from the steel frame. I rushed in and found my husband almost in a coma. I had all the arrangements for a drip. With the eager helping hands of my neighbors, I set up the drip. Silently, I thanked my teachers, who had taught me the most efficient method of finding the vein and inserting drips or injectables. Soon, my husband was back with us, though he had no recollection of what had happened.

After this harrowing episode, everyone advised us to change the wooden door and get a steel door with a mesh in addition to the wooden door. This door would have a lock that could be opened both from the inside and the outside. Both of us then decided that whenever my husband was alone at home, he would never latch the door but lock it, so that if any problem arose, I could open the door with my key and enter the house. It was also decided never to latch the wooden door.

On that fateful day when Amit was standing at the door, my husband had forgotten these instructions. He did not latch the wooden door and kept it open, but he latched the steel door instead of locking it. Thereafter, the demon of low blood sugar caught hold of him.

The saga of breaking doors does not end here. There was another episode, this time in Bengaluru, where I was transferred in March 2005 as the Deputy Medical Superintendent, ESI Hospital Rajajinagar, Bangalore,

Karnataka. My husband retired on February 28, 2005, and accompanied me to my new posting.

I usually did not allow my husband to travel alone because I feared for his safety. Having faced so many episodes of near disaster, I was wary of leaving him alone, especially on trips. However, he had to visit Delhi urgently for some work. I had a very important meeting that could not be missed and thus could not leave Bengaluru. My husband insisted that he would be able to manage alone. He promised to take good care and abide by the rules and instructions I had dictated. I agreed reluctantly, and he went to Delhi by air. He was to return on the third day, which he did, declaring to me, "You don't trust me, but I have managed alone and returned safely." I was happy for him as it boosted his morale, and I was a bit reassured about his safety.

My husband had returned early that morning, having taken a late evening flight with a few hours' stopover at Mumbai. We had breakfast together. I cooked lunch for him, placed it on the kitchen counter, and departed for work. My husband planned to rest after breakfast.

By this time I had been promoted to the post of State Medical Commissioner, ESIC, Karnataka, and was responsible for the smooth functioning of all the ESI dispensaries, as well as ESI hospitals of Karnataka. I was busy and engrossed in work, but an inner voice whispered to me around 12.30 P.M. It was possible that my husband, who had been awake the entire night, would be in a deep slumber and not wake up for lunch. This would spell disaster. He had taken his insulin injection with breakfast and had to eat on time. I decided to ring him up. Sure enough, he did not pick up the phone, even though I called repeatedly for about five minutes. I grabbed my bag and rushed home in my car. By this time, I owned a Nokia mobile phone. I was also aware that the ESI hospital was nearby. On my way home, I telephoned the hospital authorities to send an ambulance because I thought it may be required.

I reached home and knocked, but as I had feared, there was no reply. I was at a loss. This was a government flat, not my own, and the door would have to be broken open. I tried to knock on the doors of a few of my neighbors, but it was futile—the husbands were in the office, the children at school. Only the wives were at home, incapable of solving the problem. Most of them spoke Kannada, and I knew only a few words of that language.

However, God Almighty has a way of coming to my rescue. The son of one of the neighbors was at home, having taken leave from his graduate school. The ambulance had still not reached, and I had no way of knowing how long my husband had been suffering from hypoglycemia. Unlike my Delhi neighborhood, the neighbors here were new and were not aware of my husband's health issues.

After some persuasion and explanation, the boy agreed to break the door down and was successful in doing so. I rushed in, and sure enough, my husband was lying in bed, drenched in sweat, cold and clammy. I immediately gave him the glucose injection, praying that he would open his eyes. He did so after some time, and I thanked the Great and Benevolent God who had once again come to my rescue. The ambulance arrived thereafter, but I sent it back as it was not required. Repairing the door took a while, although I must say that the Bengaluru authorities were very helpful, and my neighbors cooperated in every possible way.

Another unforgettable episode has now been added to our already colorful life!

## Prevention

A person is at risk of developing diabetes if they are overweight and have a family history of diabetes.

People who have high cholesterol levels or are pre diabetics—having blood sugar values a little higher than normal—are also at a greater risk of having diabetes.

Those who lead a sedentary lifestyle and do not exercise at least four to five times a week also risk developing diabetes, especially if they are above the age of 45–50 years.

Here are some ways of preventing diabetes, whether you have a genetic predilection for this disease or not.

1. Eat healthy: Add more fruits, vegetables (especially non-starchy vegetables), nuts, and whole grains to your daily diet. Avoid/restrict consuming fast food, oily and fried dishes, and high-calorie food.

2. Exercise regularly: Aim for at least for 30 minutes a day, a minimum of five days a week.

3. Maintain your weight within the normal range for your age and height.

4. Get your blood pressure checked regularly and ensure that it is within normal limits.

5. Get your cholesterol levels checked regularly and discuss with your doctor if they exceed normal limits.

You may still develop diabetes if you have a genetic predisposition or develop insulin antibodies for some reason, but maintaining a healthy lifestyle by following these guidelines will ensure that it is well controlled, and you will avoid developing complications.

# Resistance and Reminiscence

*"In the depth of winter, I finally learned that within me there lay an invincible summer."*

—Albert Camus

Diabetes, and especially diabetes of a brittle nature that requires constant vigilance, leads to a life of colorful episodes. The supporting group of helpers, supervisors, friends, and colleagues needs to pitch in from time to time to maintain the precarious threshold of life in such a patient. Besides major incidents that could occur despite constant care and vigilance, the daily routine may have several bumps and hiccups too, which are sometimes upsetting, sometimes hilarious, and sometimes downright frightening.

During my husband's work life in Indian Airlines, his colleagues, subordinates as well as supervisors, had become super-vigilant. After his diagnosis in 1984, my husband worked for 20 years and received several promotions, ultimately retiring from the highest post, as Director Jet Shop. During his posting at Indian Airlines House, the official headquarters of the organization, from the late 1980s to late 1990s, his assistant was always extra cautious about his mealtimes. Even during important meetings, he was apt to interrupt and remind my husband about taking his meals before anything untoward happened. Despite this protective vigilance around him, several minor and major incidents occurred at his office.

My husband is a very punctual person. In fact, his entire family has a fetish for punctuality, and I admire them for it. My father was never on time though my mother was the exact opposite. She could not abide anyone who was not on time and instilled in us the importance of punctuality.

I am digressing. This tale is about my dear husband. He always reached his office on time and carried food to be eaten at regular intervals. However, important work would interrupt this schedule quite often. Once, he was sitting in his room after a meeting when a junior colleague came to discuss an issue that had cropped up. He found my husband staring into space, not responding to his queries, but smiling and laughing instead. Suspecting a problem, he telephoned the doctor whose office was located two floors below.

Dr. Jaichand rushed upstairs, and assessing the situation, he prepared a drink of glucose and asked my husband to drink it. My husband refused, pursing his lips. The poor doctor scolded and cajoled him for several minutes, but when he did not cooperate, he threatened my husband with hospitalization. Ultimately, when he was about to get the injectables, miraculously my husband opened his mouth and gulped down the drink. The level of blood sugar had not dropped too drastically, because this glass of glucose did the trick. Within 10 minutes, my husband was feeling better. By this time, the word had spread through the office like wildfire, and several people had peeped in to view the proceedings. Everyone breathed a sigh of relief as things returned to normal.

Despite our best efforts to ensure regular mealtimes, monitor blood sugar regularly, and ensure that he always carried enough food, including sweets, major and minor incidents of hypoglycemia became the bane of our life.

Another incident occurred at the office sometime later. This one had a more lasting and disastrous impact. One morning around 11 A.M., my husband had an attack of low blood sugar but did not realize it. He was walking back to his room from the restroom when there was a sudden crash. He had fallen in the corridor. Others immediately rushed to his aid and he was carried to his room, as his eyes were blank and he was unable to walk. The doctor rushed to his cabin and gave him a glucose injection, which revived his blood sugar. However, he started complaining of pain in the region of his right shoulder. Suspecting a fracture, the doctors decided to shift him to the hospital for further investigation and treatment. However, someone had to be with him while he was in the hospital.

Dr. Jaichand, who also stayed in Saket and knew me well, got my office landline number from my husband and contacted me. A senior colleague in my office received the phone call—all of us were not provided with direct external phone lines and were connected by an internal network of phones. My senior called me on the phone. After getting apprised of the details, I was naturally very upset. I took a half-day off and drove to the hospital where his doctor had taken him. The ever-vigilant Dr. Jaichand handed him over to me after narrating the events of the morning and his suspicion of a fracture. X-rays at the hospital revealed a partial fracture of the greater tubercle area of the humerus. A plaster cast was applied to the upper arm, and we headed home. The healing of the fracture took its own sweet time. One cannot rush nature; it heals and heels perfectly with adequate care, but the healing takes its own course. My husband took some time off from his office but joined back later, supervising and conducting his work through dictation and telephone.

After the healing of the bone, there followed months of physiotherapy to ensure proper movement of his right shoulder joint. The efforts were successful, but this was not the only episode when my husband required extensive physiotherapy.

Several minor incidents kept occurring at his office, but they were promptly attended to, averting any major problem. One such incident occurred while he was on an outstation tour to interview new recruits for his company. The team was at Jabalpur and after interviewing the students at the university, he slumped down during lunch, staring blankly. His colleagues, who were aware of his problem, took prompt action and his condition stabilized.

If nature goes against you, other humans often take advantage of the situation. When you are facing a low point in your life, there are some who will lend a helping hand and lift you, while there are others who will revel in your downfall and try to ensure that you remain there. An illness should normally not be the reason for judging performance at work, but human nature has many frailties. One of them is jealousy and the desire to succeed. My husband, with his brilliant track record in academics and excellent performance at work, had impressed his seniors and many of them loved him, having taken him under their wing. He had thus been lucky to receive a few opportunities to represent the company at prestigious occasions. Perhaps these were the reasons for instilling jealousy in the hearts of his colleagues, some of them his seniors.

When the opportunity for the next promotion arrived, despite his excellent performance, his name was dropped from the list of those promoted, stating his illness as the reason. This was blatant discrimination. However, God comes to the rescue of those who are righteous. It so happened that for some reason or the other, that list could not be operated for one year, and it expired at the end of that period. The interviews for promotions were held again, and my husband's name was on the list this time. We later learned that one of his senior colleagues in administration, Mr. P. N. Sinha, and a few others had played a role in ensuring fair treatment. My husband survived the discriminatory treatment, but sadly, others are not so lucky and suffer throughout life, often becoming despondent.

Another major incident was not a side effect of low blood sugar but was the product of our joint stupidity. At the back of our little flat is an open area, called *angan* in Hindi. It is too small to be a regular *angan*, but we use it for storage and to dry clothes. For our safety, this area is covered with a steel latticed screen so that its walls cannot be jumped over. The covered screen has a trapdoor to access its roof for cleaning and other purposes. Foolishly, we had a straight stepladder to climb to the trapdoor. This step ladder would have to be balanced against the wall, and one person held it while the other  climbed up to lock or unlock the trapdoor.

One evening, we opened this door to inspect something, and then we had to close and lock it. I held the ladder, and my husband climbed up to lock the trapdoor. However, while he was climbing down, the ladder slipped on the marble floor. I was unable to control or stop the fall. My husband fell on the glass door of the nearest room, along with the ladder. The glass broke. As my husband was trying to prevent his fall by holding onto that door, the glass pierced his right hand near the outer edge, toward the little finger. Blood gushed out in spurts. I was aghast and guilty. I bandaged his hand with swathes of cotton and bandage, and we rushed to the nearest hospital. The orthopedic surgeon was available, so we did not have to wait. After the necessary investigations, my husband was taken to the operation theater for stitches because the gash was deep and had cut through his tendon. Unfortunately, the surgeon missed the ends of the tendon while stitching up the muscle, fascia, and skin. Thus, when the wound healed, my poor husband was unable to bend his little finger!

There was nothing to be done. A second operation was not warranted as the ends of the tendon had retracted. The only alternative was physiotherapy. My husband's cousin is an excellent physiotherapist and a very sincere one, not sparing her patients, or even her brother. We visited her regularly for almost a year, daily after dinner. She often chided my husband for not making any effort himself, but the fruits of her labor paid off. My husband was eventually able to bend his finger, and it healed to complete normalcy. There is no noticeable trace of that accident now, but it did give us a scare at the time. However, persistence and physiotherapy paid off.

Physiotherapy has healed my husband and me umpteen times, and over the years, I have become an ardent admirer of physiotherapists and their trade.

Popping a pill is not always the solution. Getting agitated and frustrated too is not the answer. Some cures take time. I have had to learn this lesson the hard way, because I am a person who suffers from anxiety and is apt to lose direction in my agitation. My husband is the one who calms the tumultuous clouds of my active imagination, analyzing, reasoning, getting to the root cause, and solving the problem with persistence and skill.

## Holistic Management

Diabetes can affect every part of the body, sometimes early, sometimes after years of living with the disease. It is therefore important that the patient not only takes care of medication but also keeps an eye on every part of the body.

Long-term diabetes can affect many systems of the body, disrupting the balance. It is thus imperative that the patient, in conjunction with the primary care provider and any other family members assisting at home, ensure that the following habits are a part of life:

1. Check blood sugar daily if on insulin, and periodically, at prescribed

intervals, from the laboratory, whether on insulin or on oral medication.

2. Ensure meal intake at regular intervals, keeping an interval of 3–4 hours between meals. Light snacks may be required between meals, especially in the case of insulin-dependent diabetics. A balanced diet, containing proteins, carbohydrates, and fat, is ideal. Consult a dietician in case of any doubt.

3. Take regular walks or do yoga or other exercises daily, or at least five times a week, for 30–40 minutes. If there is an injury or pain in any part of the body, consult a physiotherapist.

4. Get glycated hemoglobin tested at prescribed intervals.

5. Schedule a complete blood analysis periodically for other important data, such as liver function tests, kidney function tests, thyroid hormones, cholesterol levels, and any other blood analysis required.

6. Schedule a periodic urine analysis to ensure kidneys are functioning well.

7. Get regular eye checkups, at least once a year.

8. Look for signs of any pain, swelling, tingling, or other discomfort in the feet, legs, and hands. Seek a consultation from a doctor well versed in dealing with these issues if you find any signs.

9. Regular blood pressure monitoring is important. Seek cardiac consultation if advised by the primary care provider.

10. Male patients should look for any signs and symptoms of prostate enlargement and seek consultation if required.

11. Get proper sleep at regular times.

Diabetes is not just a disease; it becomes a lifestyle and must be managed accordingly. Consider it your friend, and not your foe.

# Diabetes Is Not the Lone Devil

*"It is during our darkest moments that we must focus to see the light."*

— Aristotle

We were sitting quietly and watching the activity around us. Nurses rushing around in their crisp uniforms. Doctors entering or exiting, stethoscopes dangling from their necks or stored in their scrubs. My heart was filled with anxiety, as I am sure it was my husband's, but as usual, he was calmer than I was. We were at the reputed Rajeev Gandhi Cancer Institute in Delhi, awaiting our turn to be summoned by the doctors for my husband's biopsy.

The year was 2003. It was the month of April, and for the past few months, my husband had been experiencing increased frequency of micturition. He had to make very frequent trips to the restroom to pass urine. His nightly sleep was often disturbed by the urge to evacuate his bladder. He was loath to consult anyone but, on my persistence, he had consulted the doctors in his office. They had referred him to a reputed urologist who was on his office panel, and we had met him a week ago. The doctor's diagnosis was that my husband's prostate was enlarged. This was not the problem. The good doctor had also found the prostate to be slightly irregular at one place. He thus referred us for the special transrectal ultrasound required in this case.

Keeping our fingers crossed and praying, we got the ultrasound done. It displayed some frayed, unclear shadows in the central part of the prostate, sinking my spirits to the lowest. Dr. Anupam Bhargava, the urologist, then referred us for a biopsy and here we were, awaiting our turn.

At the Rajiv Gandhi Institute, prostate biopsies were conducted as an OPD procedure, unless otherwise indicated. We sat, surveying the activity around us, apprehensive of what awaited us. At last, my husband's name was called, and he went into the mini outpatient procedure room. The doctors refused to let me in as a precautionary measure to avoid extraneous infection. It was a quick procedure, and he was out within 20 minutes, but he was dizzy and weak. He rested for another 20 minutes, as advised, popping a few sweets for sustenance. The initial plan was that he would drop me off at my office and then proceed to his office at the Indian Airlines headquarters. However, he was in no position to drive, and his lunchtime was nearing. Luckily, we had packed lunch with us. We went to the car, and I took over the driving seat, but not before he had eaten.

The roles were reversed: I dropped him at his office and then went to mine. I was hesitant, but my husband insisted that he was fine, especially after resting and eating. Skeptical and fearful, I complied because both of us had important afternoon meetings at our respective workplaces. I had an office event in the evening too, which I could not miss. I went for it, anxiety and fear gnawing at my heart.

Two days later, the report was ready and could be collected personally. Rajeev Gandhi Cancer Institute is almost 35 km from our residence, so it was decided that while my husband attended the office, I would go alone to collect the report.

I discussed the report with the doctor at the Institute, and he disclosed that in one of the slides, there was a slight suspicion of cancer cells. They would therefore like to repeat the biopsy after 15 days. I was devastated, but I requested them to give me the slides they had prepared. There are some perks of being a doctor! The doctors very courteously gave me the slides and agreed that I could get them evaluated by other pathologists.

From Rohini, where this institute is situated, I went to Raja Garden towards ESI Hospital, Basaidarapur. I decided to consult Dr. Aruna Sood, our senior and expert pathologist. She was very understanding and graciously agreed to examine the slides at the earliest. Leaving the slides with her, I headed to the office, as I had taken only a half-day off. Dr. Sood was busy, but she had promised to study the slides in the evening before leaving her laboratory.

I reached home, exhausted after a long day. My heart was sorrowful, fearing the unknown future, and my eyes filled with unshed tears.

This was an unexpected turn in life, and I did not know where to go from here.

Our phone was ringing at home. I picked up the receiver listlessly. It was Dr. Sood, and she sounded joyful, not morose. I perked up. She said that in her opinion, the slides were clear, and there was no evidence of carcinoma. This was music to my ears, and I thanked her profusely for her efforts.

However, we were in a further dilemma now. Two pathologists had given us two different opinions. When my husband talked to his doctors at the Indian Airlines office, they referred him to Batra Hospital for a third opinion.

The culture of multispecialty corporate hospitals had yet to gain a foothold in India, but there were a few privately owned hospitals that were run on those principles. Batra Hospital was one of them, and in those days, it was one of the renowned hospitals of South Delhi. It was also located at a conveniently drivable distance from our house. This was a boon for me. We approached the specialist there for consultation, and he advised my husband to get admitted for a repeat biopsy under anesthesia. Thus, my husband was admitted to Batra Hospital.

The biopsy was scheduled for the next morning and was performed competently under anesthesia, with sample tissue taken from multiple sites from his prostate gland.

The post-operative recovery was uneventful, although my husband was extremely irritated by the constant disturbance from nurses during the night, who came to monitor his blood sugar. I teased him that he was getting a dose of his own medicine. He had disturbed me for umpteen nights for several years! But I felt sorry for him too.

Although the official result of the biopsy reached the doctors on the third day, I made several trips to the pathology department, introducing myself and befriending the pretty, young pathologist. Luckily, all the twelve samples obtained were cancer-free, and we heaved a sigh of relief. It was a feeling of liberation and rejuvenation.

In consultation with the uro-surgeon, it was decided that his truant prostate gland, which had caused all this mischief, should be removed. It was convenient because he was already in hospital and had the mandatory referral from the authorities. We complied with the advice of the doctors, as this was the easiest and most sensible approach to solve the problem. Two days later, the transurethral resection of prostate (TURP) procedure was done successfully, ending one episode of the story of the prostate.

Our stay in the hospital continued for the next three or four days. It was generally uneventful except for an episode of severe hypoglycemia one night. The nurses came at their regular times to check on him, but there was no bedside bell for the patient to call them in case of an emergency. One attendant always stayed with the patient, and in his case, I was there. In the middle of the night, I felt that my husband was very restless. By now, I considered myself an expert in detecting hypoglycemia. I checked, and sure enough, his body was cold and clammy. In his restlessness, he was at risk of falling from the high hospital bed. I also had no sweets with me that night because I was in a hospital and had become complacent. I ran to the nursing station to report the problem, urging them to check his blood sugar and inject glucose.

The nurses promptly took the necessary remedial action, and 15 minutes later, my husband was back to normal. They were at a loss regarding the reason for the low blood sugar because he had been provided with food that had the prescribed number of calories. It was my turn to explain to them that in a brittle case of diabetes, the blood sugar decides to take matters into its own hands and makes us dance to its tune.

My husband was discharged on the fourth day with mandatory instructions. However, the surgeon cautioned us that the prostate gland is liable to grow back again in four to five years.

On February 28, 2005, my husband retired from Indian Airlines, where he had been working since 1972. As luck would have it, I received my transfer orders the next day. I was transferred to ESI Hospital Rajajinagar at

Bengaluru as the Deputy Medical Superintendent. We were in a dilemma about going. I had the option of going to Bengaluru or taking voluntary retirement. My husband had just retired, and several formalities needed to be completed; there were loose ends to be tied up. We had been living in Delhi for the past three-and-a-half decades and had our own dwelling for two-thirds of that period.

It was a dilemma that was ultimately resolved by my daughters. They advised me to go to Bengaluru and persuaded my husband to accompany me. This decision turned out to be the best one because we spent a blissful three years of our life in that city.

Life of course is not a bed of roses, and this journey has many roadblocks. In March 2006, we faced one such hurdle.

"Why is my urine so dark?" my husband had been inquiring for the last two or three days.

I promised to get his urine checked at the hospital laboratory, but somehow, the decision kept getting postponed. Then, one day, he was very disturbed. There was frank blood coming out from his urethra, and his undergarments were stained.

We did not have a separate urology department at ESI Hospital Rajajinagar in those days, so I consulted the surgeons after sending his urine sample for testing. There was nothing specific revealed in the urine, except, of course, red blood corpuscles. The surgeons examined him. We narrated the history of his past illness and the details of those episodes to them. They were already aware of my husband's diabetic status. The investigations revealed that his prostate was again enlarged, and with the frank blood in urine, they suspected carcinoma. We were back to square one, once again facing the threat of cancer.

I applied for leave and we returned to Delhi, having already fixed an appointment with Dr. Anupam Bhargava. He performed a biopsy himself this time at his nursing home. A day later, he declared that my husband was cancer-free. We had escaped the clutches of cancer again. Dr. Bhargava advised us to get a second prostatectomy done at the earliest.

As a retired person, my husband was provided with medical benefits from his organization. However, we decided to forgo the reference hospital, which was again Batra Hospital, and get the prostatectomy done by Dr. Bhargava. He was the best and most experienced expert available in South Delhi, his nursing home was very close to our residence, and the most important factor was that we had faith in him.

My husband was operated upon two days later, this time under spinal anesthesia. The entire procedure was screened on a television/computer, and my husband was able to view his own operation, something that satisfied as well as excited him, for he considers science as God. The tissues sent for pathological testing were all declared cancer-free, and everyone breathed a sigh of relief.

Sometimes, we reminisce and laugh that his organs keep playing truant one by one. The pancreas and the prostate were the chief troublemakers, vying among themselves to decide who would generate more mischief. The Ps troubled and frightened us. Perhaps because his name starts with P, the Ps danced around him rhythmically!

# Factors that Can Raise Blood Sugar

Besides the imbalance between caloric intake, output of energy in the form of exercise/activity, and availability of effective insulin in the body (naturally or through injections), there are other factors that can raise blood sugar levels.

1.  <u>Anxiety and stress</u>: They are often inevitable in life, but if you anticipate a stressful situation, try to act so that your blood sugar does not rise unprecedentedly.

2.  <u>Caffeine</u>: Consumption of caffeine, in the form of coffee, tea, or colas, tends to increase blood sugar.

3. <u>Age</u>: As the years pass and your diabetic state progresses, your blood sugar may be higher than before.

4. <u>High-protein or high-fat diets</u>: It is a myth that a diet that is high in protein or fat and low in carbohydrates can prevent the rise of blood sugar levels. If glucose is lacking in the meal, the body converts protein to glucose. Similarly, fats also lead to an increase in blood sugar, albeit over a longer period.

5. <u>Infections</u>: When there is infection in a diabetic person, the body tends to produce increased levels of stress hormones. These stress hormones can cause the blood sugar level to be very

high, thus increasing the requirement of insulin to counteract this spike.

6. <u>Inactivity</u>: Sitting or being inactive for long periods of time will cause your blood sugar to rise.

7. <u>Hypoglycemia</u>: After an attack of hypoglycemia, to compensate for the low blood sugar level, the body releases a hormone called adrenaline, which can drive the liver to produce more sugar for the body.

8. <u>Thyroid dysfunction</u>: The thyroid gland produces hormones that are required for carbohydrate metabolism. If the secretion of these hormones is disturbed because of disease or autoimmunity, it affects the

control of blood sugar in a diabetic patient.

9. <u>Medicines</u>: Consumption of some medicines such as corticosteroids, medicines for blood pressure or heart disease, diuretics, and even some antibiotics can raise the blood sugar level. The treating physician should always be made aware of the diabetic status of a patient.

# Another Cousin

*"Chalti chakki dekh ke, diya Kabira roye, do patan
ke beech me, sabut bacha na koye."*

*(Kabir cries as he watches the mill grinding grain,
for nothing stays whole in the jaws of this mill of
life.")*

– Kabir Das

His eyes were tinged with a yellowish hue,
and he was listless.

Another major health issue crept up in 2004.

In May 2004, my husband and I went to
Lucknow to attend the wedding of my niece.
Lucknow has a special place in our hearts, and
we try to visit it whenever possible. It is my
birthplace and I have a plethora of cousins,
aunts, and uncles living there. It is always a

pleasure to meet them and relive childhood memories. My husband's only sister — 12 years older than him and almost a mother figure — is married into a family in Lucknow. He too was always eager to visit Lucknow and meet his sister and her family.

We attended the marriage and revealed all the events that are an integral part of an Indian marriage. Chatting with everyone after several months or years and eating the mouth watering delicacies prepared only during Indian marriages, was rejuvenating. We spent three extremely enjoyable days in Lucknow and returned home to Delhi, joining back the grind of daily office work.

After 20 days of our return, one morning, my husband complained of passing dark-colored urine. On examination, I noticed that his eyes were tinged yellow. There was now a laboratory just next to our house, and the doctor in charge was well known to us. We went there to get his blood and urine tested, and sure enough, as I had suspected, he had jaundice. More alarmingly, he had traces of ketones in his urine. We headed to Batra Hospital once more, where, considering his diabetic status and the urgency, the doctors immediately admitted him to maintain round-the-clock surveillance. He was in good hands, and having caught the culprit at an early stage, we were feeling reassured that he would soon recover and return home.

My niece, Shalini, was helping me out. She brought homemade food for me and agreed to keep a daily vigil for half a day. I thus managed a half-day absence from work every day. Shalini usually came in the afternoons after completing her own obligations. On the third or fourth day, I had to attend an urgent meeting at the office in the morning. I requested Shalini to stay with my husband during that time.

The meeting was in full swing when my phone, which I had kept on silent mode, vibrated. It was from Shalini. I could not ignore the call, for Shalini would not disturb me unless it was imperative. When I took the call, the voice at the other end sounded desperate. "Please come immediately. I don't

know what has happened to Chachaji (uncle)."
I tried to learn more, but she was unable to explain and only implored me to come to the hospital urgently.

My heart filled with an unknown fear, I requested my seniors to excuse me and proceeded to my car. I don't remember at what speed I drove, but I do know that I was at the hospital within 30 minutes. Parking the car, I rushed to the room where my husband was admitted. The scene that met my eyes there was far from chaotic. Two doctors and a nurse were at my husband's bedside; Shalini was standing at a distance, looking scared.

One of the doctors asked me, "Where were you? He had a severe allergic reaction to the salt in the solution that was being given in the drip. If this young lady (pointing to Shalini) had not been here, we could have lost him." Filled with extreme dread, I inquired about his condition, to which he replied curtly, "Thanks to our timely intervention, he is now stable and has recovered." I breathed a sigh of relief and thanked the doctors and nurses profusely. After they left the room, I requested Shalini to tell me exactly what had happened.

"A nurse came to the room about an hour after you left. She set up and started a drip, requesting me to keep an eye on it and inform her if the drops were not flowing or the solution was about to finish. She then left the room. About 10 minutes later, Chachaji started feeling uncomfortable and started shivering.

Soon, he was rolling on the bed. I was scared and immediately rushed to the nursing station to inform them. These two doctors were coming out of the neighboring room, and I informed them too. The nurses and doctors came rushing into the room, removed the drip and gave some injections to Chachaji. Slowly, his restlessness abated, and he could talk."

As I had noted earlier, there was still no bedside bell in the room to alert the nurses or doctors in case of an urgent need, and it was considered mandatory for a patient's attendant to be in the room with the patient. This was precisely why I had left for the office only after ensuring that Shalini would be in attendance during my absence. However, it irked me that the nurse had left my husband soon after setting up the drip. Reactions to a medicine can occur at any moment; she should have stayed in the room for some time or made a visit soon after. I understood the paucity of staff and the humongous responsibility on the hospital staff, but somehow, the incident left a bad taste. I shuddered to think what could have happened if perchance Shalini had left his bedside for some time.

I have often been blamed and ridiculed for being overprotective and always hovering around my husband, not leaving him alone. However, such incidents that creep up unexpectedly have further cemented my resolve not to abandon my vigilance.

Diabetes affects every organ of the body, and one should be extremely vigilant throughout life, intercepting each little mischief maker as early as possible to avoid any catastrophe. Following the entry of this unwanted partner on our journey of life, we were, and are, constantly on tenterhooks. The devilish episodes creep up unexpectedly, in ever-changing forms, always opening a new chapter in life to suspect, avoid, or manage.

With the passage of time, the biggest hit has been taken by his teeth. It started early and although he has been visiting his dentist regularly for annual dental checkups, a few of his teeth have been extracted. After every meal, it is a 10-minute ritual for him to clean his teeth. Despite regular brushing of teeth and due care, he occasionally faces discomfort, and has had acute episodes of severe toothache, caries, gingivitis, and the like. On one side of his jaw stands one lone molar, a sentinel that has also been drilled for a root canal. It is one more witness to the rollercoaster ride that diabetes brought to our lives.

## Diabetes and the Oral Cavity

The following points must be kept in mind with diabetics.

1. Patients of diabetes mellitus may suffer from dysfunction of the salivary gland, leading to a decrease in the flow of saliva in the mouth and a feeling of dry mouth.

2. Dental caries or tooth decay is much more common in those with diabetes, especially if it is uncontrolled.

3. Dental pulp may also be affected, causing necrosis and gingivitis.

4. Gums may become inflamed (red and swollen) and bleed easily.

5. Fungal and bacterial infections of the mouth (candidiasis) and teeth are apt to develop in diabetics with poor management of blood sugar.

6. Alterations in taste, a burning sensation in the mouth, and poor oral wound healing are also some of the problems that may occur if

proper oral hygiene as well as blood sugar control are not maintained.

7. It is important to brush your teeth twice daily with a soft toothbrush that should be changed frequently.

8. Flossing of teeth at least once a day and always cleaning the mouth and teeth after meals goes a long way in preventing tooth and gum diseases.

9. Regular checkup of teeth by the dentist is recommended.

10. Smoking increases the risk of gum disease.

Teeth are important, so the teeth and mouth should be kept healthy and happy.

# Settling Down

*"I don't agree to be like other drivers; I aspire to be unique in my own way."*

– Lewis Hamilton

The scene was comic as well as chaotic. Pankaj, my son-in-law, clutching a *laddoo* (an Indian sweet) in his hand, was in pursuit of my husband. His father-in-law was giggling like a child and going around the living room, dodging Pankaj. I was surveying all this, bewildered. I would have found it comical and laughed if the situation were not so serious.

My daughter was also worried and kept calling out, "Papa, please sit down." It was all to no avail. Neha and Shaunak, my grandchildren, aged just four years and two years, were too young to understand. Their innocent brains found it a game of pursuit, and they were laughing with delight and enjoying themselves immensely, running after their father.

A few minutes ago, I had realized that my dear husband was in the throes of low blood sugar as I happened to touch his hand and found it cold and clammy. We had eaten lunch only an hour ago, and I was surprised, but not unduly so. By this time, having lived with diabetes for more than 25 years, we were all familiar with its tantrums and the hide and seek it played with my husband. We knew that blood sugar could rise and fall for a variety of reasons, not only the caloric intake.

It was a Sunday afternoon in June 2007, and we were visiting our elder daughter in Maryland, USA. We had arrived from India a couple of weeks ago. Our two grandkids were at that age when playing with grandparents was a pleasure for them, and we, as the elders, wallowed in their love and sweet cuddles. I was still working, so these visits were short. We endeavored to come at least twice a year, however, and this was the longer summer visit.

I had warned my children that their father was having an attack of low blood sugar after I noticed his hand was too cold to touch.

Unfortunately, we did not have glucose tablets handy. But a box of sweets was conveniently sitting on the kitchen counter, having freshly arrived from India. I picked up a *laddoo* from it and asked my husband to eat it, but he, in the throes of hypoglycemia, stubbornly refused to open his mouth. Pankaj then courteously decided to take the onus of feeding Papa. I handed the sweet to him, and he started persuading my husband to eat it. Suddenly, my husband leaped up, running away from him.

Now, Pankaj was in pursuit of Papa, who was giggling and going round in circles around the living room sofas. Pankaj is taller and naturally faster, so he was able to get closer, but my husband seemed to have superhuman energy and kept evading him. Suddenly, I think he had a lucid interval. He sat down and opened his mouth wide. Pankaj pushed the sweet into his mouth and my husband ate it. We waited for 15 minutes, the time it usually took for him to normalize after eating sweets, and heaved a sigh of relief when he began behaving and talking normally.

Life had settled down to a routine by now and such episodes, which were the norm earlier, had become few and far between. They had started lowering in number and settling down after the doctors changed his insulin to human insulin. After the first three to four years of injecting the porcine insulin, we noticed that my husband was not responding to it—the blood sugar level remained persistently high despite increasing the dosage. It turned out that my husband had developed resistance to that insulin. The treating doctors therefore decided to switch him to human insulin, which was easily available in India in the tenth decade of the twentieth century, in the 1990s. His body's response improved, which reduced the harrowing and unpredictable episodes of hypoglycemia considerably. The patient was thus able to maintain better and more fruitful control of his diabetes. However, freak accidents continue, and they still harass us if caution and routine are not followed. Whenever we falter, the devil steps up, punishing us with a vengeance.

Another episode, more recently in 2018, was entirely due to negligence and oversight. By then, I had retired, and we were staying with our children for much longer periods. This episode happened when we were staying with our elder daughter. It was a glorious summer day in Northern Virginia where my daughter and her family reside. As it was a Sunday, the children decided to visit the relics of the old war memorials of Virginia, located near Vienna. After relishing a lazy breakfast, everyone piled into the red van that was very handy for such occasions.

We traversed the length and breadth of the historic site, enjoying the warm sunshine and the long, lazy, but refreshing walk, engrossed in our conversation about the Civil War and its consequences. We must have walked for at least an hour and a half, strolling along, soaking in the beauty of the region, inspecting the war relics interspersed in the area. Thereafter, we got into the car and visited a nearby winery to have lunch and enjoy some wine. Both my husband and I entirely overlooked the fact that he had walked so much after breakfast and needed a more sumptuous lunch, or alternatively, a lower dose of insulin. I anyway paid scant attention to this fact because my husband had been managing his injections and medication himself for years now, and I stepped up only when required.

Over pizza and wine, we chatted happily on different topics. My husband injected himself with his usual dose of insulin, ignoring the vigorous exercise he had undertaken that day.

The insulin commenced its action soon enough. After lunch, we tarried and went around to admire the rows and rows of green and black grapes in the vineyard.

On our way back home, I noticed that my husband was unusually quiet. Suspicious, I touched his hand and found it cold and clammy.

I asked whether he had brought his glucose tablets and looked in all his pockets, but he had none. I then frantically examined my bag because I generally kept a pack there. But I was carrying a different bag that day, so it had no glucose tablets. None of us had any food to help raise his blood sugar. Prabhat was talking normally and insisting that he would be alright, and we should head straight for home. So, Pankaj continued driving.

However, insulin and blood glucose levels wait for no one. They follow their own agenda. By the time we reached home, his blood sugar was very low. He faced inordinate difficulty in getting out of the van and reaching our bedroom. Prompt action to feed him was taken, but I regretted the lapse on my part—forgetting to ensure that we had sufficient ammunition to fight the devil of hypoglycemia. We also made a tactical mistake in not stopping and buying some sweets.

I recall another such incident, which happened purely because of our lack of vigilance. While in Bengaluru, we took a short trip to

Hyderabad in March 2007 to meet my school friend, Ranjona. We have been friends since Class 8, and our husbands too have become very friendly with each other. Ranjona and I were busy gossiping and catching up with various aspects of our lives. We ate a sumptuous breakfast of *idli* (steamed cakes of rice and lentil) and *sambhar* (a tangy lentil soup with a variety of vegetables and spices). Lunchtime was nearing, and I looked toward my husband. He was not sitting where I'd seen him last, and Suren, my friend's husband, informed me that he had wanted to rest and was in the bedroom.

My senses immediately went into emergency mode. This was such an unusual occurrence. When I went to examine him and call him for lunch, I found him drenched in sweat. His eyes were blank, and he was not responding coherently. Both of us had overlooked his midmorning snack time and now he was in the throes of hypoglycemia. Although we had glucose tablets, he was past the state of ingesting them. My second mistake was that we had not packed glucose injectables and equipment.

Ranjona's house was on the third floor. My husband had to be carried to the elevator to be driven to the hospital. With the help of her two adult sons, we reached the hospital in time. He recovered soon after the glucose drip started, but I kicked myself for being so inattentive toward the needs of our third partner and endangering my husband's life.

We are very thankful that such episodes are rare now. My husband leads a normal life for the most part, and despite the compulsory nuisance of injecting himself morning, evening, and after every meal, life is sedate and peaceful. Episodes of hypoglycemia are few and far between. Still, the recent episode in 2018 jolted us, reminding us not to let our guards down.

## Role of the Caregiver (Hospital/Clinic)

Diabetes is best managed by the patient themselves. It is therefore essential to empower the patient by explaining the various facets of the disease in simple language. The educational and mental level of the patient must be kept in mind while laying out the facts in a simple, precise, and firm manner.

If the patients are able and willing to learn a few basics of the body's functions and the nature and cause of the ailment that has afflicted them, the facts should be laid on the table for the patient to comprehend. Be gentle and tolerant but persistent. Let the patients ask as many questions as they want to, so that doubts and fears are allayed and it is understood that this is a lifelong problem and should be handled with care.

Side effects and consequences of not adhering to the prescribed diet and exercise schedule and skipping medication must be explained firmly and with clarity.

If the patient is unable to take care of themselves, the accompanying family member should also be apprised of all the facts with instructions on the patient care schedule. This is extremely important for patients who are taking insulin.

All the signs and symptoms of hypoglycemia should be explained. The procedures of dealing with hypoglycemia correctly must be emphasized.

Carrying glucose tablets or other sweets is a requirement, and this must be explained to the patient and the caregivers. It may mean the difference between life and death.

# The Expert

*"Do not go where the path may lead. Go instead where there is no path and leave a trail."*

−Ralph Waldo Emerson

When the demon of diabetes struck our lives, my husband was completely unfamiliar with this word and ignorant about the disease and its ravages. Over the years, this has changed dramatically.

Let us begin from the beginning about the man I loved and chose as my life partner. By all accounts, he was a math Mad Hatter from childhood, calculating and solving math problems at every opportunity. It could be at school, while doing his homework, on a slate, on a wooden pellet we used during our childhood, a notebook, or even the floor with chalk. Any instrument of writing was his ammunition to defeat math puzzles. When depressed or angry, I was told, the avenue he sought to overcome his frustration was solving math problems all over the floor of the house.

Born to simple, devout parents, who never went to school but were self-taught, Prabhat, my husband, was their last child, arriving seven years after his youngest brother, almost as an afterthought. His father was a businessman and mother an extremely efficient lady, the inspiration behind the success of every child. They had four surviving sons and one daughter, the apple of her parents' eyes. My husband's sister was 12 years older than him and was almost a second mother in his life.

This math maniac, my husband, was a brilliant student and went on to secure the fourth position in the list of candidates selected in the prestigious All India entrance test for the renowned Indian Institutes of Technology (IIT) in 1963. He joined the institute of his choice, IIT Kharagpur, then considered the best in India.

Although the bane of his life was English, a compulsory subject in first year, he passed with flying colors in every other subject and was amongst the nerds of his batch. He completed his B. Tech. degree in July 1968 and later joined M. Tech. at IIT Kanpur, but two months before his final examinations in 1970, he received a very lucrative offer for the prestigious post of an engineer in the domestic national airline, Indian Airlines. On the advice of his professors, he joined the airline, forgoing the final examination.

We met in 1972 and married with the blessings of our families in January 1973. My husband was very successful in his career and loved his work. His seniors appreciated his precision, foresight, and work ethic. His subordinates loved him as he was an excellent teacher, patient and caring, always ready to explain and assist anyone who wanted to learn and master the intricacies of aircraft and their engines. Overcoming the inevitable hurdles and competitiveness that are bound to happen in every career, he rose to the level of Director Jet Shop. This Jet Shop serviced the jet engines of the various aircraft in the Indian Airlines fleet. He managed to make several major and credible improvements in the Jet Shop, raising it to international standards. He retired from Indian Airlines after a successful stint of 34 years.

My husband is a man of firm convictions and strong principles, and he is a firm believer in the magic wielded by science. Although he has no faith in religion, he indulges me and participates in all the rituals I perform during Indian festivals. He tackles every problem with the exactitude and precision of a scientist and a mathematician, not being swayed by emotions or hearsay. Precision, patience, and persistence are his mantras for succeeding. I am just the opposite, getting worried, anxious, and impatient. He thus becomes my rock of stability whenever I falter. My unshakable faith in the Supreme Power, the influence of my grandparents and parents, especially my father, also helps me.

After retiring from Indian Airlines, my husband delved in the stock market, a passion that has continued till today. While I was pursuing my master's degree in public health at Washington University in St. Louis, he took classes at the H&R Block to learn about the system of US tax evaluation and calculation, and he now manages all these affairs expertly for both of us.

Throughout the 50-plus years of our journey together, he has been my rock of Gibraltar. I can always lean on him and be assured that any issue that has cropped up will be resolved with his expertise. He uses the same proficiency and craftsmanship to manage his health issues. Since diabetes is a disease that affects the entire body sooner or later, he has been ensuring that each part is taken care of. Nowadays, he contacts his primary care provider at the first sign of trouble, asking for advice and following the guidance given.

Despite good care, this Shylock has extracted his pound of flesh. My husband developed high blood pressure about five years ago and has been on medication for it since then. At first, it was one drug in small doses; now, he takes two in larger doses. Very recently, he has been diagnosed with glaucoma and thus uses the mandatory eye drops advised by the ophthalmologist. When the eyes are afflicted, how can the ears be left behind? He has become hard of hearing and uses hearing aids.

Sometime back, he started experiencing pain in his knees, especially the right knee. On examination, I found a soft mass behind his knee, which turned out to be a popliteal cyst, also commonly known as the Baker's cyst (after the surgeon Dr. William Morrant Baker who first described it). Cold compresses, rest, and physiotherapy have alleviated his pain and discomfort, but the cyst persists. It is now another item to be taken care of with hawk-like observation and monitoring. Despite constant care and precautions, he has now developed the same problem in the left knee. The doctors have declared him as having arthritis, the inevitable friend of old age. Regular ingestion of calcium and Vitamin D is added to the list of daily medical requirements.

A very old friend, the inguinal hernia, has revisited him after all these years, this time on the right side. It is a direct inguinal hernia and is being managed with a belt at present. In due course of time, surgery may or may not be required.

His blood tests also reveal that he has mild hypothyroidism and fatty liver. The gradual decline in vitality and the problem of sleeplessness have also appeared in his life. We can blame both aging and diabetes for all these additions, but he exercises, monitors, reads, analyzes, and manages his insulin injections, all with the precision of a scientist, after understanding all the pros and cons of the issue concerned. For better control of blood sugar, the tablet metformin has also been prescribed by doctors now, thus increasing the variety of his medicine cabinet.

An example of his expertise lies in the management of his insulin doses and injections. Barring a few initial doses, he learned to inject insulin himself soon after it was prescribed to him. As time elapsed, he managed well and started scrutinizing and questioning the dosage prescribed. He surmised rightly that one hat fits all could not be the prescription rule, and every human body should be reacting and responding differently. The requirement of insulin has increased almost tenfold since his initial diagnosis, perhaps because production from the pancreatic factory has gradually declined and shut down almost completely over the years.

Initially, he was required to inject long-acting insulin only once a day. It increased to twice a day very soon, and now, my husband also takes short-acting insulin with every meal. His prescriptions changed from long-acting to

NPH insulin, to short-acting and long-acting combined. Experiments were also done with a brand containing premixed insulin, a mixture of long-acting and short-acting insulin, but this was not effective. Now, he is required to take a shot of Humalog (short-acting) insulin with breakfast, lunch, and dinner and NPH (longer-acting insulin) before bedtime and with breakfast. Although the doctors have prescribed fixed amounts, the bolus of insulin required to be injected must often be calculated depending on the intake and activity as well as the results of the sugar analysis. It is impossible for any human being to eat the same amount and same type of food, day after day. Nor is it possible to be consistent with exercise every day. He has been prescribed doses by his doctor, but it often falls upon my husband to carefully evaluate and calculate the amount of insulin to be injected.

We noticed a peculiar phenomenon in his readings around 2010. His early morning readings were not very high, wavering between 110–150, sometimes lower, but they increased drastically two hours later, by breakfast, sometimes to alarming levels beyond 300. During this interval between waking up and breakfast, he consumed only a cup of sugarless black coffee and a cup of black tea without sugar. He also practiced yoga for one hour. We had consulted several specialists in India, but none of the solutions offered were helpful.

Three years ago, he consulted his primary care doctor in the USA and was advised to take a single dose of long-acting insulin before going to bed. My husband noticed that this dose was not effective in maintaining a consistent level of blood sugar by the next afternoon. The readings tended to rise despite increasing the dose of post-lunch short-acting insulin. He is a member of an online insulin takers' group, where members often exchange notes of their experiences. Some of them advised dividing the long-acting insulin into two doses, half before bed and the other half before breakfast. This was very effective in balancing the afternoon readings, but the mystery of the unprecedented increase in readings just before breakfast lingered unresolved. Recently, pondering over the problem, my husband himself decided to shift the dose of long-acting insulin that he took before breakfast. He opted to experiment by taking the long-acting insulin just after waking up and testing his blood sugar. Viola! The problem appeared to be resolved. He was elated that at last, his thoughtful analysis and expert scientific thinking were able to help him.

In 2023, we returned to India from the US toward the end of July. My husband had read a lot about the device for continuous glucose monitoring. He wanted to try it, although I was hesitant. I was apprehensive of a skin reaction due to excessive sweating in the intense heat and humidity of Delhi. His persistence and firm belief in science and its wonders won the battle of wills. After due search, online as well as through contacts, the device was purchased and installed. As usual, he was right. It has proved extremely useful and helps in averting attacks of hypoglycemia, because it informs and warns the patient when the blood sugar is following a downward trend. This is thus the latest addition to the multiple tools in the diabetic kit. Sometimes, both of us wish that some of these wonderful new technologies had been available when he developed diabetes. Life would have been much easier and smoother to manage.

This stubborn but gentle, quick to flare up but caring and loving, intelligent and hardworking gentleman has been my life partner, along with the unwanted visiting companion, his diabetes.

## Role of the Caregiver (Home)

Diabetes is a disease that is best managed by the patient themselves, for the patients know their body best. The patient is aware of what they eat, when they rest, what exercise they undertake, and the patient is the one who faces firsthand the fluctuations of glucose levels, the dance of insulin, and the pain of the setbacks due to this unexpected visitor that has entered their life.

The caregivers at home have at best a supportive role to play:

1. If you are responsible for preparing meals for a diabetic family member, it is best to acquaint yourself with the specific caloric requirements of the patient, based on age, exercise level, and general lifestyle.

2. Prepare a chart or spreadsheet for the different meals of the day on different days of the week. This must be done with as much precision as possible, calculating the caloric needs as per the advice of the doctor and the dietician.

3. Meals require variety, despite the diabetic menace, and exchange food with as much exactitude as possible should be prepared.

4. Emergency telephone numbers to be contacted should be handy and displayed at a place where all the members of the household can access them easily.

5. Sweet drinks, candies, or glucose tablets must be readily available. If the patient is a child, the caregiver must carry these when traveling or visiting. Blood sugar levels vary, increasing and decreasing drastically, owing to many reasons besides food.

6. Infections of any form in the body may cause the blood sugar to remain high. The caregivers at home should be aware of this and help the patients to

treat their infections as early as possible.

7. Encourage the patient to take regular exercise, accompanying them whenever possible.

8. Learn to detect the various signs of low blood sugar so that you can assist in prompt and early remedial action.

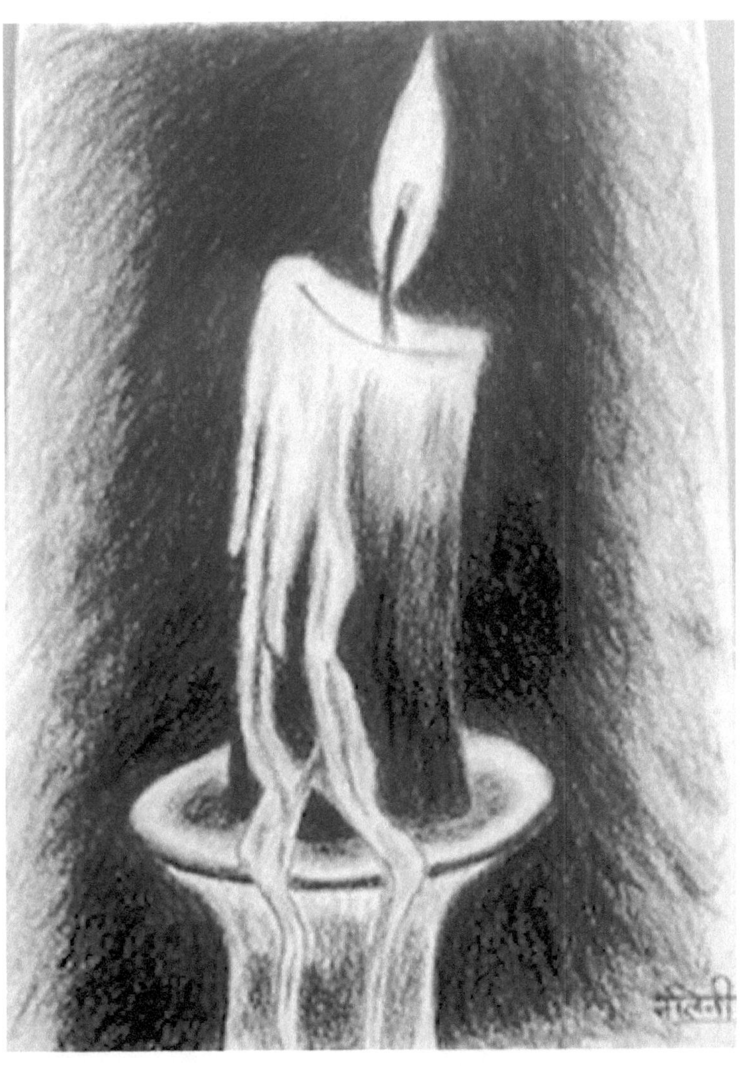

**The Candle of Life Burns Yet, With Hope
and Glow!**

# Epilogue

This journey of life with my diabetic husband has been a seesaw of ups and downs, but we have both coped and managed to survive with aplomb despite the often-unprecedented hurdles. We brought up two wonderful daughters who have made us proud of their achievements. They are both settled in the USA with their brilliant and incredibly understanding husbands and are managing their families well. We have also been blessed with four amazing grandchildren, who provided immense joy when they were younger and are a source of pride for their parents and grandparents.

I have toured the world with my partner, and my children. Before the menace of diabetes joined our journey, I took my first airplane ride with my husband, visiting Jammu and Kashmir and filling my memory album with the entrancing beauty of Srinagar, Pahalgam, and Chandanwadi. The hike to Vaishno Devi on our way back was a bonus.

The next trip was with friends to Bengaluru, Mysore, and Hyderabad. We were unaware then of what destiny had in store for us. We later spent three blissful years of our life in Bengaluru, touring the length and breadth of Karnataka as well as many parts of the other three South Indian states.

Our life, with all its ups and downs, has been a blessing, and its rollercoaster rides, though scary at times, have been rejuvenating. We have been very fortunate, and if I start counting and lining up my blessings, the result would be more than a mile long. We have traversed the length and breadth of India. Of the 29 states and Union territories, we have managed to visit and explore almost 20. We have also completed the pilgrimage to the four sacred places in four corners of India: the Char Dham Yatra.

Besides India, we have also explored the wonders and beauty of monuments, parks, and cities of almost 20 countries in Asia, Europe, North America, and South and Central America. When I look back, I find it amazing that despite the sword of constant vigilance hanging over our heads, we achieved so much in our lives.

Our children, friends, family, and even strangers have all pitched in to help when required: cooperating, understanding, tolerating our weird schedules and demands, and accommodating us and our needs.

I have often wondered why my husband developed diabetes. Since there was no history of diabetes in his family, after ample contemplation and discussions with physicians, the only possible reason for his ailment seems to be an autoimmune response destroying the beta cells, making his body lose the capacity to produce insulin. There is a history of other types of genetic diseases in his family, and sometimes I wonder if he had the genetic predisposition for this change. My husband's paternal grandfather died very early, when my husband's father was just 3-4 years old. Having no knowledge of the cause of his grandfather's death, I speculated whether he had diabetes and died of its complications.

Recently, another thought struck me. His brother, Ganesh Bhai, was unlike his other siblings. He could not even clear high school while the others were all postgraduates and brilliant students. Ganesh Bhai died very early, in his late 30s, after a very short illness that affected his kidneys. Before the illness could be properly investigated or diagnosed, he was no more. Ganesh Bhai had two sons: the elder, Anuj, has gluten allergy, and like his father, could not clear high school. The younger one, called Ashu, was diagnosed as having a rare genetic disorder called tuberous sclerosis that can affect one or multiple organs of the body with benign growths. This child's growth was in the brain and affected him severely, making him wild, unpredictable, and difficult to manage. He passed away in 2005 at the age of 35 years.

I had taken Ashu to AIIMS in 1983, and his diagnosis was explained to me by the neurologists there. I tried to read more about it, but I had no access to the Internet and the vast array of information now available on computers. The books I had access to had very little information about this disease. I wondered if the disorder was in the family but brushed the thought aside because there was no other known case.

Recently, the thought struck me again. My husband was advised to have an ultrasound of the abdomen by his physician. When the result arrived, it indicated two small benign fatty growths on his kidneys, labeled as hamartomas. Curious, I read about them and discovered that they occur because of tuberous sclerosis. This disorder can cause such growths in any part of the body and can also lead to autoimmune reactions in the body. Waves of doubt assailed my brain. Did my husband develop diabetes due to an autoimmune reaction caused by tuberous sclerosis complex?

Is my husband's diabetes an offshoot of a genetic problem affecting his family, which is handed down to sons? I am not an expert, and this needs to be put forth before knowledgeable endocrinologists. This thought perhaps leads to my labeling his diabetes as brittle diabetes and latent autoimmune diabetes of adults (LADA), which surfaces generally after the age of 30.

When I contemplate the reasons for his developing diabetes, so many possibilities occur to me. Was the damage to his system due to his twice developing severe typhoid of long duration in childhood, or was it the combined effect of prolonged pesticide spray in our apartment (for almost two years) as well as the new medicine given by the physician for his constipation? Did the continuous high fever he suffered in 1983 at Bareilly affect his system, or were the shocks of events in 1983–84 responsible? All these thoughts invaded my psyche at different intervals, though I curbed them because my saner reasoning said that these alone could not be the culprit. Now, after the details discovered in the ultrasound report, the cause appears more plausible.

We will never know the truth, and perhaps that is best for all of us.

The multiple, and often life-threatening, problems we faced at the onset of diabetes could have been due to various circumstances. The factors that I always seem to enumerate include the type of insulin given to him not being very effective or suitable for his needs. Moreover, during the early stages, the pancreas may have been sporadically secreting some insulin, upsetting the balance of insulin in the body and the amount required by it. At the time, we did not have the sophisticated monitoring equipment available later. Thus, frequent checking of blood sugar with accurate results was not possible.

We can speculate all we want, but the fact remains that he has a very brittle type of diabetes that took time to settle down in tune with our lives, aided by the gradual introduction of sophisticated testing and treating techniques. Even now, no one can sit back and relax. Constant vigilance, monitoring of blood sugar, and balancing the intake of food with the output of energy is an ever-present necessity. I sometimes think that managing a Type 2 diabetic, whose ailment behaves like Type 1 diabetes, is like dancing a delicate ballet. If the coordination is correct, you strut along perfectly on your toes. If you falter, you fall flat and endeavor to balance again.

# A Note About the Diabetic Diet

Diet is an extremely important aspect of managing the complex phenomenon of diabetes. Thus, dear readers, it is only befitting to add a separate note about this special and important aspect of managing diabetes.

The mantra of the diabetic diet is that everything should be partaken in limited quantities—protein, fat, and even healthy carbohydrates, or carbs. Let us understand what healthy and unhealthy carbs are.

Healthy carbs encompass all the whole grains, like brown rice, *chana*, *daliya* (broken wheat), oats, whole wheat bread, quinoa, barley, and all millets. They have more fiber and take longer to digest, thus raising the blood sugar level gradually.

Unhealthy carbs are *maida* (refined flour) and everything made from *maida*, all deep-fried dishes, such as *pooris, bhaturas, samosa, kachori,* and so on. Naan, cream biscuits, white bread, and all sweets also provide us with unhealthy carbohydrates. They satisfy our taste buds but lead to a sharp spike in blood sugar, which is dangerous for diabetics. Thus, these should be completely avoided or severely limited.

Sugars are now labeled as the new cancer for the body. White sugar is bad, but brown sugar, honey, agave, jaggery, and other sources of sugar are all as good or as bad as sugar. Coconut sugar should also be avoided. Date sugar, on the other hand, has a lower glycemic index, which means it is better for the body when compared with other types of sugar. In simple terms, when a food has a high glycemic index, it raises your blood sugar at a faster rate to a higher level after consumption.

Dairy is also not good for sugar control. Dairy includes not only milk but also cream, cheese, butter, ghee, mayonnaise, ice-cream, *kulfi*, full fat yogurt, and other dishes made from milk. Hence, all these foods should be avoided.

Every region of India has its own unique cuisine, and it is difficult for people originating from a particular region to change their eating habits completely. That is neither desired nor feasible. Here are a few guidelines for the

Indian population, especially those who are vegetarian, and have diabetes or prediabetes:

1. Eat more proteins in the form of all kinds of legumes, such as dals, *rajma, kala chana,* or *lobia.* These can be cooked with less oil or ghee. You can also soak and sprout or boil them to incorporate into salads. Another variation would be to soak and grind them or dry powder and mix them with whole wheat flour or rice flour to prepare roti, *dosa,* or *cheela.* Enterprising cooks also prepare pizza out of this dough adding only sauces and vegetables or meat.

2. Eat green vegetables daily, cooked or in salads.

3. Eat fresh fruits, especially those that are non-starchy and less sweet, such as berries, melons, oranges, and so on. Avoid fruits that are rich in sugar content. Although fructose, the sugar in fruits, is better than cane sugar and easier to digest, it has a high glycemic index and raises the blood sugar. Thus, fruits like sweet mangoes, grapes, sweet watermelon, sweet apples, bananas, and so on should be avoided or eaten in limited quantities.

Eat only whole wheat bread and boiled potatoes (never fried).

Consume nuts but in limited or prescribed quantities.

The only dairy item that can be consumed daily is yogurt prepared from reduced fat milk. All other dairy products must be avoided or taken in limited amounts. Milk, if necessarily required to be taken, should be reduced fat milk.

Other food items that are good for a diabetic are roasted *chana* as snack, sprouts, vegetable-stuffed roti with no oil, clear soups, and unfiltered vegetable juice (use tomatoes, spinach, gourd, or bitter gourd). A quick, healthy snack is to mix roasted chana with a little puffed rice *(lai or layya)*, add a drop of mustard oil and some chat masala, and toss well. Chopped cucumber or onion pieces can also be added to this snack for extra taste and bulk.

All processed juices and cold drinks should be completely avoided. Homemade *nimbu paani* (lemon water) with a little salt should be consumed instead.

Alcohol consumption should be avoided completely or limited to a glass or two per week.

Drink tea and coffee without sugar and preferably without milk. Lemon tea is good.

The general rule should be to choose foods that have a medium or low glycemic index. Fresh vegetables and fruit should be consumed. Meals should be cooked using less salt and less oil, butter, or ghee. Roasting and boiling vegetables are the most effective methods of reducing overall calorie intake. Meal quantities should be kept under control.

As a rule, the meal of a diabetic should have a quarter plate of salad, another quarter of cooked vegetables (prepared with less oil), a third quarter of dal or other form of protein, such as chicken, fish, paneer (made from reduced fat milk), legumes, *rajma/chole*, or yogurt. Only one quarter of the plate should have carbs in the form of whole wheat bread, roti, *cheela*, *dosa*, *idli*, etc.

Living by these principles of diet, combined with adequate age-appropriate exercise helps. It is challenging but well worth it to pacify the diabetic devil and enjoy a complication-free life.

# My Husband then and Now

# Acknowledgement and Appreciation

The idea of this book had been lingering in my mind for a long time. However, it was the prodding of my two daughters, Geetika and Geetanjali, that instigated me to act and pen down my thoughts. Geetika, who is a good writer herself, encouraged me to make several improvements at various junctures of this book. Both Geetika and Geetanjali also assisted me by going through the script and helped me to recall various events. Without their persuasion and assistance, this book would not have taken its present shape. I am indebted to both my daughters.

I am also thankful to my husband, Mr. Prabhat Narain Tandon, who jogged my memory and helped me to recall several episodes of our journey together, especially those related to his office life.

I am extremely grateful to Mrs. Pratibha Pandey who has designed the cover of my book. She is an eminent and accomplished artist and despite her busy schedule she helped me with this project. I am indebted to her.

I must thank Shamenaz, a dear friend who is the author/translator of several books and the director of PLCS literary society. She has been actively instrumental in getting this book published. Shamenaz you are ever ready to help and encourage.

Last, but not the least, I am very grateful to Pragya, my editor. Her patience with my various just and unjust requests, as well as my repeated additions and deletions, must have tried her patience. She tolerated them all, and persisted in editing my work, correcting, improving, and bringing it to its present shape.

Thank you, Pragya!

# About the Author

Dr. Nalini Tandon was born in Lucknow and spent her childhood and teenage years at

Allahabad. After passing Class 12, she completed her Medical Studies from Lady Hardinge Medical College. Completing her residencies two years later, she worked with ESI Corporation for 34 years, retiring in 2009.

Thereafter, she shifted to the USA and obtained a master's degree in public health from Washington University in St. Louis. After working in the USA for a few years, she retired and revived her childhood desire to write poems and stories.

She is the author of *We Were, We Are,* her memoirs, and *Yaadon Ki Pankhuriyan,* a collection of poems. She has also edited two of her father's books and got them published.

She lives in the USA and India and spends her time writing, painting and traveling the world.

## References

Bliss, M. (1984). *The discovery of insulin*. University of Chicago Press.

Cleveland Clinic. (n.d.). *Insulin*. https://my.clevelandclinic.org/health/body/22601-insulin

Da Silva Xavier, G. (2018). The cells of the islets of Langerhans. *Journal of Clinical Medicine, 7*(3), 54. https://doi.org/10.3390/jcm7030054

DiGiacinto, J., & Higuera, V. (2023, April 20). *Everything you need to know about insulin*. Healthline. https://www.healthline.com/health/type-2-diabetes/insulin#takeaway

Garg, S. K., Kipnes, M., Castorino, K., Bailey, T. S., Akturk, H. K., Welsh, J. B., Christiansen, M. P., Balo, A. K., Brown, S. A., Reid, J. L., &

Beck, S. E. (2022). Accuracy and safety of Dexcom G7 continuous glucose monitoring in adults with diabetes. *Diabetes Technology & Therapeutics*, 24(6), 373–380. https://doi.org/10.1089/dia.2022.0011

Hirsch, I. B. (2018). Introduction: History of glucose monitoring. In the Role *of Continuous Glucose Monitoring in Diabetes Treatment*. American Diabetes Association. https://doi.org/10.2337/db20181-1

Jurca, C. M., Kozma, K., Petchesi, C. D., Zaha, D. C., Magyar I., Munteanu, M., Faur, L., Jurca, A., Bembea, D., Severin, E., & Jurca A. D. (2023). Tuberous sclerosis, Type II diabetes mellitus and the PI3K/AKT/mTOR signaling pathways — Case report and literature review. *Genes*, 14(2), 433. https://doi.org/10.3390/genes14020433

Karamanou, M., Protogerou, A., Tsoucalas, G.,
Androutsos, G., & Poulakou-Rebelakou E.
(2016). Milestones in the history of diabetes
mellitus: The main contributors. *World
Journal of Diabetes*, 7(1), 1–7.
https://doi.org/10.4239/wjd.v7.i1.1

Mandal, A. (2023, July 4). *History of diabetes.*
News-Medical.Net.
https://www.news-medical.net/health/Hi
story-of-Diabetes.aspx

Mohan, V. (2023). National diabetes prevention
programmes in LMICs are now a necessity.
*The Lancet Global Health, 11*(10),
E1480–E1481.
https://doi.org/10.1016/s2214-109x(23)003
81-9

Polonsky, K. S. (2012). The past 200 years in
diabetes. *The New England Journal of*

*Medicine, 367*(14), 1332–1340.

https://doi.org/10.1056/NEJMra1110560

Raza, S., Raza, S., Kazmi, M., Saad, M., & Hussain, I. (2021). 100 years of glucose monitoring in diabetes management. *Journal of Diabetes Mellitus, 11*, 221–233.

https://doi.org/10.4236/jdm.2021.115019

Scheiner, G. (2020). *Think like a pancreas: A practical guide to managing diabetes with insulin.* Hachette Go.

Talathi, S. S., Zimmerman, R., & Young, M. (2023). *Anatomy, abdomen and pelvis, pancreas.* StatPearls [Internet].

https://www.ncbi.nlm.nih.gov/books/NBK532912/

Titchener, J. (2020). Diabetes management: A manual for patient-centered care. CRC

Press.
https://doi.org/10.1201/9780429326196

Watkins, P. J., Drury, P. L., & Howell, S. L. (1996). *Diabetes and its management.* Wiley-Blackwell.

Zazworsky, D., Bolin, J. N., & Gaubeca, V. B. (Eds.). (2005). *Handbook of diabetes management.* Springer.

www.ingramcontent.com/pod-product-compliance
Lightning Source LLC
Chambersburg PA
CBHW051219130726
47988CB00001B/141